AIR FRYER Cookbook

BEST HEALTHY, EASY AND QUICK RECIPES TO FRY, GRILL, BAKE, AND ROAST WITH YOUR AIR FRYER

Written by Linda Croll

TABLE OF CONTENTS

AIR FRYER COOKBOOK...1

INTRODUCTION 6

THE BASICS OF YOUR AIR FRYER 8

AIR-FRYING: STEP BY STEP...9
WHAT AILS US 10
EATING HEART HEALTHY 10
TRIM THE FAT—AND SALT 14
OTHER DIETS AND HEART HEALTH 14
CHOOSE WISELY 15
VERY VALUABLE VEGGIES..16
SEASONAL EATING 16
WHEN TO GO ORGANIC...20
SAFETY 21
TROUBLESHOOTING..22
CLEANING AND CARING 23

BENEFITS OF THE AIR FRYER 25

WHY YOU SHOULD USE AN AIR FRYER ?....................................27

QUESTIONS AND ANSWERS 28

TOP TIPS FOR USING THE AIR FRYER 30

BREAKFAST RECIPES 33

Breakfast Potato Gratin 33
Potato Bites with Cheese 34
Air Fryer Spinach Frittata 35
Easy Breakfast Casserole 36
Delicious English Breakfast 37
Healthy Breakfast 38

BREAKFAST SANDWICH 39

MAC & CHEESE WITH TOPPING 40

TOASTS WITH CHEESE 41

BAKED EGGS IN AVOCADO NESTS 42

FRIED EGGS WITH HAM 43

SANDWICH WITH PROSCIUTTO, TOMATO AND HERBS 44

FRENCH TOAST STICKS 45

CHEESE OMELET 46

DUTCH OVEN BAKED FRENCH TOAST WITH EGGS 47

SHIMEJI MUSHROOM OMELET 48

FRENCH TOAST STICKS 49

BUTTON MUSHROOMS WITH PARMESAN 51

FRITTATA WITH SAUSAGE AND PARMESAN 52

RED PEPPER SOUFFLÉ 53

EUROPEAN BREAKFAST 53

CREAMY MUSHROOMS 54

SAVORY OATMEAL WITH BEANS AND PEPPERS 55

SPICED TOAST 56

HAM AND EGG CROISSANTS 57

BACON AND EGG BREAKFAST SANDWICH 59

PARMESAN TOAST 60

APPETIZER 61

FETA PASTRIES 61

MUSHROOM AND ONION CROQUETTES 62

CHEESY POTATO BALLS 63

FRIED FISH FILLETS 65

VEGETABLE PAKORA 66

POTATO AND PARMESAN CROQUETTES 67

SAVORY STUFFED MUSHROOMS WITH PARMESAN 68

RICOTTA BITES 69

GREEN BEANS WITH SHALLOTS AND ALMONDS 70

PIZZA WITH PEPPERONI 71

FETA PILLOWS 72

Classic Spring Rolls...73

Delicious Breaded Mushrooms 74

Crunchy Jalapeno Peppers..75

Baked Cheesy Crescents..76

Roasted Pepper Rolls with Feta.....................................77

Rice and Vegetable Stuffed Tomatoes.........................78

Broccoli with Cheddar cheese 79

Asparagus Spears Rolled with Bacon 80

Mushrooms Stuffed with Garlic.....................................81

Appetizing Fried Cheese 81

Stuffed Mushroom Caps...82

Melt-in-Mouth Salmon Quiche with Broccoli 83

Mini-pigs in Blankets 84

Spicy Grilled Tomatoes 85

Cheeseburger 85

LUNCH RECIPES...86

Mushroom Cordon Bleu 87

Zucchini & Tuna Melts..88

Carrot Noodles 89

Stuffed Spinach Leaves...90

Deluxe Stuffed Zucchini 91

Spiced Stuffed Peppers 92

Spinach & Feta Pastry..93

Ham & Cheese Balls 94

Easy Air Fryer Pizza 94

Simple Beef Burger 95

Turkey Rolls...97

Broccoli Bacon Burger 98

Turkey Stuffed Bell Pepper 99

Hot & Sweet Ham Sandwich...100

Bean & Turkey Bacon Burger 101

Chicken Pita Sandwiches 102

AIR FRYER DINNER RECIPES...103

TURKEY BREAST WITH MAPLE MUSTARD GLAZE 103

GENERAL WONG'S BEEF AND BROCCOLI 104

IRRESISTIBLE MEATLOAF 106

ROCKSTAR RIB EYE-STEAK 107

25. UNIMAGINABLE ZUCCHINI BACON LASAGNA 109

FANTASTIC GARLIC BUTTER PORK CHOPS 110

SUPER-YUMMY ROAST PORK BELLY 111

OUTSTANDING RACK OF LAMB...112

PHENOMENAL HERBED ROAST BEEF..114

REMARKABLE AIR-FRIED HAM WITH HONEY AND BROWN SUGAR GLAZE 115

AMAZING LAMB CHOPS WITH HERBED GARLIC SAUCE......................................116

ROASTED LAMB RACK WITH A MACADAMIA CRUST 118

AIR FRYER MEATBALLS..119

MARINATED ROSEMARY ZEST TURKEY BREAST 121

HONEY GLAZED PORK RIBS 122

AIR FRYER BAKED BEEF AND POTATOES 123

SPICY MASALA BOTI 124

CRISPY PORK ROAST 125

HOT SHOT FACTIONS 126

CONCLUSION 127

Introduction

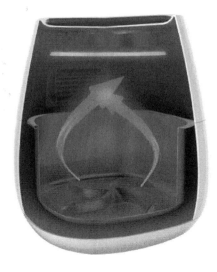

The air fryer is latest multipurpose kitchen trend. It gives every household the ability to cook food in a fast and easy when making their everyday meal. The air fryer's specific design is to function without the use of fattening oils while cooking foods with at least 80% less fat. Thus, the air fryer can truly help you shed excess poundage that you have been longing to lose completely.

The air fryer allows you having all the food you like to eat despite having difficulties of letting go of your favorite and craved about fried dishes! Exactly, you may still enjoy your fried dishes while conserving at the same time all those saturated fats and calories. As you plan switching into a healthier lifestyle, the air fryer offers the perfect kitchen must have appliance for you.

This new technology makes it possible to fry, bake, toast, steam, and grill food by a single machine. The other main advantage of this super innovative machinery is to use a very small amount of cooking oil compared to other existing fryers. The method is to use very hot air to cook food in a just few minutes in a healthier way, because it only requires a very small amount of oil even for frying food. Plus a drip tray is inserted into which the fryer basket is fitted in order to cook crunchy and pleasantly golden food.

With the air fryer, each and every contemporary and traditional dish can be made very easily, like chicken, fish, beef, vegetables, patties, cakes, pastries, meatballs, kebabs, turkey fajitas, cupcakes, muffins, chips, quiches, cupcakes, toasts, burgers, macaroni, curly fries, mousses, puddings, scones, biscuits, and much more in a single pot without any mess and with very little effort.

This machinery is highly valuable for those who want to cook food easily in just few minutes and without so much struggle and mess all over in the kitchen. You can make food with your air fryer that was not imaginable before the introduction of this great device.

Moreover, this equipment is very effective to prevent numerous cardiovascular diseases, due to very less amount of cooking oil usage. So cooking in air fryer is indeed a healthier way for those who love fried and toasted foods but are very conscious about the high intake of oil and fats.

Air fryers were launched in early 2010, first in Europe and later Australia, then in Japan and North America. Air fryers have become a necessity cooking appliances nowadays in most contemporary kitchens.

The Basics of Your Air Fryer

One of the best tools that you can bring into your kitchen is the Air Fryer. If you are a fan of all things fast food, the tasty chips, the breaded chicken, and all that delicious goodness, but are worried about the fats and oils that come from deep fat frying, the Air Fryer is the choice for you. Rather than using hot oils to produce the good foods, such as fish, chicken, chips or pastries, the Air Fryer will utilize hot air to cook the meals.

This makes the food taste just like it would if you used a deep fat fryer, but with a lot less oil thanks to using the hot air inside the machine, you are eating something so much healthier for you. Add on that the Air Fryer usually takes just a few minutes to cook up these meals and you can have a mouthwatering meal in front of your family in no time.

The Air Fryer is going to use a grill as well as a fan to blast really hot air around your food at high speeds. This will achieve the effect of crisping and browning around the food, such as what happens when you bake, toast, or fry the food, but since you are using really hot air to cook the food rather than lots of hot oil, you are getting a healthier option with all the great tastes.

AIR-FRYING: STEP BY STEP

You can think of an air fryer as a miniature convection oven. Inside the air fryer, a heater underneath the food heats the air. A slotted pan over the heater lets the superheated air move quickly around the food. A fan keeps the air circulating, and a vent pulls moisture and cooler air out of the appliance so the temperature inside stays high and constant.

Just as in deep-frying, a crust immediately forms on the food in the air fryer. This helps seal in moisture so the interior of the food can cook. The starches inside the food gelatinize, the proteins denature, and the fiber softens as the outside browns—all fancy terms meaning the food cooks as it heats.

Most recipes for air fryers are very similar to recipes cooked in ovens or deep-fried in oil. But there are some essential differences.

• Batter: Hot oil instantly solidifies a batter. But in an air fryer, the liquid runs off in the few seconds in takes for the air to heat it. Wet foods will not work in an air fryer.

• Shape: Cut foods into similarly sized pieces so everything cooks evenly in your air fryer.

• Coatings: Foods coated with bread crumbs, ground nuts, or grated cheeses should be moist enough to ensure those small particles stay on the food and do not drop off into the air fryer and burn.

Once the food is prepared according to the recipe, the air fryer is usually preheated following the instructions that came with your appliance. The food is placed in a basket and inserted into the air fryer before you start timing. In just a few minutes, out comes perfectly cooked, hot, crisp food that is ready to eat.

Good Health Begins with Your Heart

Heart disease is the number one killer in the United States. A diet high in fat and sodium and low in nutrients and fiber can contribute to this epidemic. Changing how we cook the foods we enjoy can play an important role in reducing our risk of developing heart disease.

WHAT AILS US

You've heard the saying "If Momma isn't happy, nobody's happy." For our purposes, let's amend that to "If your heart isn't happy, your body isn't happy." Many ailments that Americans struggle with have a direct impact on heart health. Obesity, high blood pressure, and inflammation can all contribute to heart disease.

The foods we choose to eat directly affect our health. Consuming too much sodium can increase the risk for developing high blood pressure. Eating too much of the wrong types of fat can contribute to obesity. And chronic low-grade inflammation, which is the body's way of responding to foreign invaders such as viruses, can lead to plaque development that clogs your arteries. These ailments can also increase your risk of stroke, diabetes, and even cancer. By focusing on keeping your heart healthy, you automatically decrease your risk of developing other debilitating diseases.

EATING HEART HEALTHY

There are many definitions of the word healthy as it pertains to food and your diet, depending on your health concerns and dietary needs. Some people reduce their carbohydrate intake. Others eat only organic foods. Some eliminate entire categories of foods, such as dairy, grains, or legumes.

In this book, we abide by the American Heart Association's (AHA) definition of nourishing, healthy food: *low in fat, high in nutrients and fiber, and low in sodium.* While the AHA no longer recommends a low-fat diet, it does say that Americans should replace saturated fats and trans fats with healthier fats such as monounsaturated and polyunsaturated fats. Most adults should consume about 13 grams of saturated fat a day, which, on a 2,000-calorie-a-day-diet, is 5 to 6 percent of calories from saturated fat. And the AHA recommends the acceptable macronutrient distribution range, issued by the Health and Medicine Division, part of the National Academies of Sciences, Engineering, and Medicine, in 2002. This recommended range, for adults, is 20 to 35 percent of calories from fat.

One tool in the AHA's recommendations is DASH—Dietary Approaches to Stop Hypertension. Hypertension, or high blood pressure, is known as the "silent killer" because usually there are no symptoms. Many Americans don't even know they have it. Thus, the AHA recommends consuming no more than 2,300 milligrams of sodium per day, and preferably 1,500 milligrams per day or fewer. To put that in perspective, one-quarter teaspoon of salt contains 575 milligrams of sodium.

Sugars are another concern. Eating a lot of sugar can increase your risk for heart disease and contributes to inflammation in the body. There are three kinds of sugar:

1 **Glucose:**

the main building block of carbohydrates

2 **Fructose:**

the sugar found in fruits

3 **Sucrose:**

granulated sugar

Most recipes use two kinds of sugar:

1 Naturally occurring sugars (fructose) from fruits and some vegetables

2 Added sugars

Most added sugars in American diets are in soft drinks, candy, cakes, cookies, pies, and some dairy products such as sweetened yogurt. Those sugars have no nutritional value other than calories. Added sugars include brown sugar, white sugar, honey, molasses, and corn syrup; those products have lots of sucrose.

The AHA recommends that men limit their intake of added sugars to 36 grams (9 teaspoons) per day; women should limit their intake to 24 grams (6 teaspoons) per day.

Naturally occurring sugars, such as fructose, are not as bad for you as added sugars. Those natural sugars come packaged with lots of vitamins A and C and fiber. And the fiber helps slow your body's processing of sugar, which decreases the rate at which your blood sugar rises. That may help prevent the development of diabetes.

The AHA also recommends that Americans reduce the number of calories they eat. Most people should eat about 2,000 calories a day, depending on age, sex, and level of physical activity. You should eat a variety of foods, with an emphasis on fruits and vegetables, whole grains, lean meats, poultry, fish, low-fat dairy products, nuts, legumes, and vegetable oils. Choose foods that are high in fiber, avoid trans fats (more on this fat later) and saturated fat, and cut back on sugar consumption.

On this diet, every day, you should eat:

. Dairy (low fat): two or three servings

. Fats and oils: two or three servings

- Fruit: four or five servings

- Vegetables: four or five servings

- **Meat, poultry, and fish:** *six or fewer servings*

- Grains: about six servings

And, if you are serious about improving your health, it's worth your while to make sure you understand exactly what a "serving" is (see Resources, here). Most Americans think a serving is much larger than it actually is. For example:

- Bread: One serving is one (1-ounce) slice.

- Fruit: One serving is one piece.

- Ice cream: One serving (sadly) is just ½ cup.

- Meat: One 3-ounce serving is about the size of a deck of cards.

All recipes included in this book have, per serving:

- No more than 35 percent of calories from fat

- No more than 140 milligrams of sodium per serving

- Only 1 to 2 grams of saturated fat, in most cases

- No more than 22 grams of sugar (most have much less)

- No trans fat

- Healthy amounts of vitamins and fiber, when possible

TRIM THE FAT—AND SALT

It's not difficult to cut down on fat and salt in your favorite foods; it just takes a little knowledge and effort.

Did you know that most sodium you consume is in packaged and processed foods? Reduce sodium by

- reading the labels and buying low-sodium versions of your favorite foods.

- choosing whole foods, such as fresh tomatoes and chicken breasts, instead of a frozen chicken dinner.

- reducing or eliminating salt added to recipes you cook. Sprinkle a tiny bit of salt on your food right before you eat it—the flavor will be more apparent, and you will be more satisfied.

To cut fat from your diet, trim visible fat off meat, remove the skin from poultry before cooking it, and choose lower-fat products, such as turkey sausage instead of pork sausage. And, again, read labels when buying processed foods and choose low-fat options.

OTHER DIETS AND HEART HEALTH

The main dietary approaches to good heart health include the DASH diet, on which this book was based; plant-based diets such as vegetarian and vegan; and the Mediterranean diet, which emphasizes whole foods, fresh produce, and olive oil. All these diets are compatible with the recipes in this book.

You Are What You Eat

Plainly put, your body reflects what you put into it. If you eat a lot of foods high in fat, your body may contain more fat. If you eat a lot of sugar, your blood sugar levels may rise. And if you consume many foods high in sodium, your blood pressure may increase. Think of food as the building blocks for your body. It's much easier to say no to those deep-fried French fries if you know that the fat will travel to your heart where, it will, ultimately, do damage.

CHOOSE WISELY

In the supermarket, not all ingredients are created equal. The nutritional difference between a cream puff and a tomato is obvious, but there's also a big difference in nutrition between a fresh red bell pepper and a wrinkled tomato. Withered produce not only looks unappealing, but it also has fewer nutrients than produce that is plump and heavy, and it may harbor more bacteria. Look carefully at everything you pick up before you put it in your cart.

Quick Picks

When you shop, look for certain things to get the most nutrition for your money:

1 In the meat department, look for plump meats, poultry, and seafood with little fat and a fresh, clean aroma.

2 Always check dates on packaged foods for the best quality. If you buy packaged greens, for instance, select the package with the date furthest in the future.

3 Read labels. Choose foods that adhere to the AHA guidelines—low in fat, high in nutrients and fiber, and low in sodium.

4 In the produce aisle, choose heavy fruits and vegetables with smooth skin and no blemishes, cuts, soft spots, or bruises. The color should be deep and even.

Ripe fruits should give slightly when gently pressed with your fingers, but they should not be overly soft. They should be heavy for their size, too.

VERY VALUABLE VEGGIES

This book's recipes use basic vegetables that are available at any grocery store and are key to a healthy diet. These foods are high in nutrients and have very little sodium and fat.

SEASONAL EATING

You may notice the inclusion of "season available" in the table that appears below. Seasonal eating is also important to good health. Fruits and vegetables have a higher vitamin content when you eat them in season; they are fresher because they haven't been shipped long distances to get to your plate, so their taste and nutrients haven't decreased. These foods lose nutrients as soon as they are harvested.

In the summer, of course, fresh produce is readily available everywhere. But in the fall and winter, many brightly colored fruits and veggies you see in the store have been shipped from miles away.

VEGGIE	HOW TO PURCHASE	MAIN NUTRIENTS	NUTRIENT BENEFITS	SEASON AVAILABLE
Asparagus	Buy asparagus that is firm and unbruised with tips that are tightly	Contains vitamins C and K and fiber	High in saponins, which are anti-inflammatory	Spring

	closed.			
Bell peppers	Look for brightly colored peppers that are firm with smooth skin.	Good source of vitamins A and C and carotenoids that give the vegetable its amazing color	Carotenoids act as antioxidants with strong cancer-fighting properties.	All
Broccoli	Choose broccoli heads that are heavy, with tightly closed florets that are a deep green color.	Good source of vitamins A and D	Contains many compounds that help prevent cancer, such as indoles and sulforaphane	All
Carrot	Choose carrots that are firm, brightly colored, smooth, and not wrinkled.	High in vitamins A and C, potassium, and fiber	Good source of fiber	All
Garlic	Look for firm heads with no soft spots.	Good source of vitamins C and B and copper	Contains allicin, which helps lower cholesterol	All

Leafy greens	Should be brightly colored with no bruises or broken leaves	Lots of magnesium and iron; low in carbs	High in fiber and vitamin C, which help protect heart health	All
Mushroom	Mushrooms should be firm and evenly colored, with no bruises or dark spots. Look for tightly closed caps.	Good source of vitamins B and D and minerals	Contains lots of vitamin D, which helps protect bone health	All
Onion	Buy firm, heavy onions with tightly attached skin.	Polyphenols and flavonoids; also high in biotin, manganese, vitamin B6, and potassium	Contains antioxidants such as quercetin that help prevent inflammation	All
Sweet potato	Look for heavy, firm sweet	Good source of vitamins A and B and	Contains lots of fiber that helps reduce	Fall Winter

	potatoes with no soft spots or bruises.	manganese	blood sugar levels	
Tomato	Buy firm, heavy tomatoes with smooth skin and no soft spots or bruises.	Great source of vitamins A and C and lycopene	Antioxidant that can help lower cholesterol levels	Summer Fall

To get the most nutrients from your foods no matter the season, consider these guidelines:

- In summer: Go crazy cooking with just about every fruit and veggie on the shelf. This is peak season for fresh berries, corn, tomatoes, and other soft fruits and vegetables.

- In fall: Rely on leafy greens, sweet potatoes, pears, squash, cauliflower, and mushrooms.

- In winter: Eat Brussels sprouts, oranges, apples, and sweet potatoes.

- In spring: Select asparagus, artichokes, peas, spinach, and strawberries.

WHEN TO GO ORGANIC

And here's an interesting question: Should you buy organic foods? Organic foods are those that are grown without artificial fertilizers, pesticides, and herbicides. Unfortunately, the produce in most American grocery stores is grown using conventional methods, and pesticide residue has been measured on many of these foods.

Some consumer advocates have created a list of the "cleanest" and "dirtiest" fruits and vegetables at the supermarket (see Appendix B, here). If you are concerned about pesticide residues on your foods, buy these five foods organically grown, if you can:

1. Apples

2. Peaches

3. Celery

4. Tomatoes

5. Bell peppers

Healthy Oils

Some recipes in this book use a tiny bit of oil to help foods brown and crisp. Any oil will work, but some are better than others. Because the temperature inside the air fryer can be set up to 400°F, only use oils that have high smoke points. That is the temperature at which the oil begins to break down and release smoke.

The oils with the highest smoke points include:

1. Corn

2. Extra-light olive

3. Grapeseed

4. Peanut

5. Safflower

All these oils are unsaturated, which means they fit into the American Heart Association's guidelines for a healthy diet. And not one of them contains any trans fat, a type of artificial fat that is particularly bad for your heart.

One of the healthiest fats for cooking is olive oil, because it can increase good cholesterol and reduce bad cholesterol in your blood. Olive oil may also help you reduce the risk of developing type 2 diabetes and stroke.

Air Fryer Safety, Troubleshooting, and Care

The air fryer is a very safe appliance because the cooking process takes place inside a sealed container. But, as safe as this appliance is, you must still handle it with care. Before you begin any cooking, read the instruction manual that came with your specific air fryer for basic safety tips and instructions on use.

SAFETY

Always place the air fryer on a stable, heat-proof surface. Don't use an extension cord to plug it in. While the fryer is operating, steam that can burn comes out of the vents—stay away from these vents while the fryer is operating. Some additional tips to stay safe:

. Be careful when removing the basket from the air fryer; it is very hot.

. Do not tip food out of the fryer, because the pan may contain hot oil or liquid. Tipping it may splash that liquid onto your hands.

. Never press the button that holds the basket and pan together when you remove them from the air fryer.

Safety also includes food safety. Always cook ground meats to an internal temperature of 160°F, pork to 145°F, chicken to 165°F, and fish to 140°F. Check these temperatures with a meat thermometer.

TROUBLESHOOTING

All air fryers are a bit different, so always read the instruction manual that came with your machine. Each brand may suggest different cooking times and temperatures for different types of cooking and foods.

My top tips for troubleshooting:

- Sometimes you must manipulate the food while it cooks. Shake the basket or turn larger foods, such as steaks or chicken, to make sure they cook evenly.

- Not crisp? If the food does not crisp, it may have been too wet. Pat foods dry before putting them into the basket. Coating some foods, such as marinated meat, with cornstarch or flour can also help them crisp up.

- White smoke that appears as the food cooks means that foods are too wet; some of that smoke is probably steam or from tiny particles of food stuck to the inside of the fryer.

- Black smoke is a sign of a problem. If you see black smoke, immediately turn off the machine, unplug it, let it cool, and take it to an appliance repairman.

CLEANING AND CARING

The manual that came with your air fryer will discuss how to clean and care for it. To clean most fryers, unplug and let the machine cool. Remove the basket and pan and wash them with soap and water using a plastic scrubbing brush—never use steel wool. If food is stuck onto these pieces, soak them in warm water for about 10 minutes before washing with soap and water. Some parts of your air fryer may be dishwasher safe; check the manual before cleaning this way.

After each cooking session, check inside the appliance for stray crumbs or bits of food and remove them. Wipe the outside and inside of the appliance with a damp paper towel or sponge. Finally, check the bottom of the machine. If there is any grease or oil there, soak it up with paper towels and wipe it clean with a cloth.

About the Recipes

The recipes in this book were chosen for their nutrient density, adherence to AHA guidelines, ease of preparation, and quick cooking. With very few exceptions, you'll be ready to eat in 30 minutes or less, start to finish. And almost every recipe requires no more than eight everyday ingredients to prepare (not including cooking spray to prepare the pan, a small amount of water needed for cooking, or optional accompaniments). All recipes include nutritional information, and each is labeled with a few defining words to help you choose, including

- Family Favorite

- Fast (ready to eat in 15 minutes or less, start to finish)

- Gluten Free

- No Sodium (fewer than 5 grams of sodium per serving)

- Vegan (no animal products)

- Vegetarian (may include dairy, eggs, or honey)

-

Very Low Sodium (recipes with less than 35 grams of sodium per serving)

Some recipes transform foods traditionally deep-fat fried into healthier options, while other foods are baked, grilled, roasted, or stir-fried to demonstrate how versatile your air fryer is.

Each recipe has a set upper limit on the amount of fat and sodium—no more than 35 percent of calories from fat and no more than 140 milligrams of sodium per serving—and includes foods that provide essential nutrients.

You can see how healthy each recipe is using the nutritional information provided, which includes

- Calories per serving

- Fat (percentage of calories from fat)

- Saturated fat

- Protein

- Carbohydrate

- Sodium, in milligrams

- Fiber

- Sugar

- DV vitamins ("DV " is the daily value of nutrients—vitamins and minerals—the typical healthy adult needs to consume every day based on a 2,000-calorie diet)

And to feel really good about these foods, 30 recipes (about one-third of the total) include a comparison called "Aren't You Glad You Didn't Deep-Fry?," which tells you the main difference between your healthier air-fried version and the traditional deep-fried preparation. Proof again, with so many recipes that are not just remade deep-fried alternatives, of how healthy this way of cooking can be.

Benefits of the Air Fryer
There are plenty of benefits that come with using the Air Fryer. Some of these great benefits include but not limited to:

- Deep oil fried taste—With the Air Fryer, you are going to get the same taste as you enjoyed from the deep oil fryer. It takes only a few minutes to make the meals and get that taste you are craving.

- All ingredients are cooked with hot air, and offer you the same great look and taste as oiled fried foods.

- The best part about not using oil is avoiding those greasy stains on your plates and fingers.

- While a little oil can be used with an air fryer, it is not common.

- When you do use oil, it is best to apply it directly to the food instead of filling the pan with a puddle of oil, since this may damage the air fryer.

- Healthier—while deep fat fried foods are great to eat, they are not so great on the waistline or for your health. When you use the Air Fryer, you are cutting the oil down and using really hot air to cook up the food, making it a healthier option while still enjoying the great taste.

- Fast and Easy: If you don't have time to make a delicious meal for the whole family. The Air Fryer allows you to get most meals done in ten minutes or less. This makes it really easy for you to get a good meal on the table with all the great taste and a reduction in the fat and valuable time.

- Many options—there are no limits to what you can do with the Air Fryer. You can cook some healthy egg options in a few minutes, great lunches on the go, dinners that the whole family will love, and even healthy desserts all inside the Air Fryer.

- Uses heat and not oil—oil is never a good thing to use in excess on your cooking. It may make things easier, but it adds a lot of calories, cholesterol, and other bad nutrients to your body. In addition, when you use a regular deep fryer, you have to worry about fires, burns, and other issues. But with the Air Fryer you will be safe.

Why You Should Use an Air Fryer ?

An air fryer can pretty much do it all. And by all we mean: fry, grill, bake, and roast.

Equipped with sturdy plastic and metal material, the air fryer has many great benefits to offer.

Air Fryers have the ability to:

- Cook multiple dishes at once
- Cut back on fatty oils
- Prepare a meal within minutes

While every appliance has its cons, the air fryer doesn't offer many.

The fryer may be bulky in weight, but its dimensions are slimmer than most fryers. An air fryer can barely take up much space of an average counter Appliances.

No Grease, No Mess

With an air fryer you can enjoy the fact that no oil is needed to cook your food. Many people enjoy the idea of eating a healthier version of normally fattening foods.

Think of it like this: No oil means no mess and less fat.

Should you decide to prepare your dish with oil, make sure you use it with homemade foods instead of pre-heated foods. Your appliance's manual should include details of which type of oils can be used with the fryer.

Questions and Answers

Question: Can we use the air fryer to cook different types of food?

Answer: Yes, you can use the air fryer to cook different varieties of food. One of the things that make the air fryer unique is that food cooked using the kitchen equipment is free of oil and healthy. Meat, potatoes, French fries, and poultry can be cooked without difficulty. Except for these food items, you can grill vegetables or bake brownies.

Question: How much power is required to operate an air fryer?

Answer: For users in the US, it is 110v, while in Europe, the input power range is about 220v, so the wattage or power consumption will be different.

Typical model of Phillip Air Fryer will be around 1425W

Question: Is it possible to cook lots of food in an air fryer all at once?

Answer: It is the capacity of the air fryer that will determine whether this is possible or not. Many air fryers come with a 500g capacity. If you look closely at the basket of the air fryer, you will notice an indicator labeled 'MAX' which imply that the air fryer should not be filled beyond this mark.

Question: Is there any special vegetable oil that is required for this fryer?

Answer: Not at all. You are at liberty to use any oil for cooking in an air fryer. Cooking oils such as coconut oil, peanut oil, olive oil, sunflower oil and even butter sprays can be employed in an air fryer.

Question: During cooking in an air fryer, can we add more ingredients?

Answer: Yes, it is possible for you to add more ingredients even when food is getting cooked in an air fryer. But ensure that you add the ingredients as soon as possible or else, the resulting heat loss will cause the food to take a longer time in cooking.

Question: What foods can be air fried?

Answer: An air fryer is a kitchen appliance that cooks by circulating hot air around the food. A mechanical fan circulates the hot air around the food at high speed, cooking the food and producing a crispy layer thanks to the Mallard effect.

Question: How many food items can one cook at the same time when using the air fryer?

Answer: It is possible to prepare two different food items at the same time in an air fryer. Ensure you make use of the divider as this will help in reducing the time it takes for you to cook and also aid proper cooking.

Question: Is it necessary to heat up the air fryer?
Answer: No, preheating is not required. Nevertheless, if you preheat the fryer for approximately four minutes, you would have significantly reduced your cooking time. There are certain recipes required you to preheat, just follow the instructions.

Question: Do air fryers help in making food appetizing and crunchy?
Answer: Yes indeed. Any food that you cook using an air fryer can be as crispy and tasty as when you fry it. This happens because of the capacity the air fryer has in making the outermost layer of the food crusty while keeping the interior parts soft but well-cooked.

TOP Tips for Using the Air Fryer
Tip 1: Many pre-made packaged food items you already purchase can be cooked using the Air Fryer. Each food may vary with its cooking time. As a guideline, reduce the cooking times by about 70% compared to times in a conventional oven.

Tip 2: When you are using lots of oil, the liquid helps your food to mix properly. That does not happen in air fryers as air is not strong enough to move the separate particles. Make sure that you are opening up the machine and mixing your food at least once when you are cooking.

Tip 3: A common mistake that many people go for is overcrowding the air fryer. Deep frying helps you to understand how much food can actually be cooked at one go via full submersion in the oil. When there is no oil, you might not leave enough space for your ingredients to be cooked properly. Make sure that you do not fall for that mistake. Did you ever hear people complaining that their air fryers cannot provide crispy results? This is usually the reason.

Tip 4: They say you don't need oil but that is not the actual case. This is basically just a marketing strategy used to promote air fryers. In reality, you need to use a small amount of oil or cooking spray to make sure you are not losing taste. Make sure you have cooking spray in your kitchen, especially for battered food that didn't come pre-oiled.

Tip 5: When working with fresh food, it's usually not a great idea to start cooking straight out of the fridge. Take your time and make sure the food you are putting into the dryer is at room temperature, this will cut down on cooking time and should lead to crisper results.

Tip 6: Though the name says 'air fryer', you should know that these gadgets can do a lot more than just frying food; you can cook everything from noodles to lasagne and even pizza. You will find a ton of options that are not remotely related to frying.

Tip 7: Make sure that you are taking good care of your air fryer. Air fryers do not need much love and attention but like an electronic appliance you do need to take care of it. If you are cooking regularly with your air fryer, try to clean it at least once every fifteen days to make sure it stays odour and smell free.

Tip 8: While cooking smaller items such as fries or wings; you can make sure they are cooking evenly by shaking the basket several times during the cooking process.

Tip 9: It is important to pat food items dry if you have marinated or soaked them in to help eliminate splattering or excessive smoke.

Tip 10: It is tempting when you are in a rush to attempt to overload the Air fryer. Don't put too much in the cooking basket at one time. You won't receive the best results if the air cannot make the 360° turns that make the cooker so unique.

Tip 11: Allow at least three minutes warm-up time each time you use the fryer so it can reach its correct starting temperature.

Tip 12: When it comes time to clean the cooking basket, loosen any food particles remaining attached to the basket. Soak each of the attachments in a soapy water solution before scrubbing or placing it in the dishwasher.

Tip 13: If you use aluminum foil or parchment paper, leave a one-half-inch space around the bottom edge of the basket.

Tip 14: Cooking sprays are an excellent choice to spray on your food before cooking. You can also spray the mesh of the cooking basket to keep anything from sticking to its surface.

Tip 15: Shaking the basket once or twice during cooking ensures that food such as croquettes, fries, and wings gets cooked uniformly.

Tip 16: Soaking the cooking basket in soapy water before scrubbing will help food particles which remain on it to come loose.

Tip 17: Some types of food may require getting them soaked in sauce or other flavorings before cooking. Ensure that you shake off excess liquid from any marinated food to prevent excess smoke or bespattering of the air fryer.

Breakfast Recipes

Breakfast Potato Gratin

Prep time: 10 minutes

Cook time: 20 minutes

Servings: 2-3

Ingredients

1 pound potato, peeled

2 oz milk

2 oz cream

Ground pepper

Nutmeg to taste

- 2 oz cheese, grated

Directions

Slice potatoes.

Combine milk and cream. Season with salt, ground pepper, and nutmeg.

Cover the potato slices with milk mixture.

Preheat the Air Fryer to 370 F.

Transfer covered potato slices to the quiche pan. Pour the rest of the milk mixture on the top of the potatoes.

1. **Evenly cover the potatoes with grated cheese.** Place the quiche pan into the air fryer and cook for 15-20 minutes until nicely golden.

Potato Bites with Cheese

Prep time: 20 minutes

Cook time: 25 minutes

Servings: 2

Ingredients

2 large Russet potatoes, peeled and cut

½ cup parmesan cheese, grated

½ cup breadcrumbs

2 tablespoon all-purpose flour

¼ teaspoon nutmeg, ground

2 tablespoon fresh chives, finely chopped

1 egg yolk

2 tablespoon olive oil

¼ teaspoon black pepper, ground

- Salt to taste

Directions

In lightly salted water boil potato cubes for about 15 minutes.

Drain potatoes and mash them finely with the potato masher. Let them completely cool.

To the mashed potato add egg yolk, grated cheese, chives, and flour.

Season the mixture with ground pepper, nutmeg, and salt.

Make 1 ½ inch balls and place them in the flour and then to the breadcrumbs.

1. **Preheat the Air Fryer to 370-390 F**

Cook potato rolls for about 10 minutes, until they become golden brown.

Air Fryer Spinach Frittata

Prep time: 5 minutes

Cook time: 10-12 minutes

Servings: 2

Ingredients

1 small onion, minced

1/3 pack (4oz) spinach

3 eggs, beaten

3 oz mozzarella cheese

1 tablespoon olive oil

- Salt and pepper to taste

Directions

Preheat the Air fryer to 370 F

In a baking pan heat the oil for about a minute.

Add minced onions into the pan and cook for 2-3 minutes.

Add spinach and cook for about 3-5 minutes to about half cooked. They may look a bit dry but it is ok, just keep frying with the oil.

In the large bowl whisk the beaten eggs, season with salt and pepper and sprinkle with cheese. Pour the mixture into a baking pan.

Place the pan in the air fryer and cook for 6-8 minutes or until cooked.

Easy Breakfast Casserole

Prep time: 15 minutes

Cook time: 25-30 minutes

Servings: 5-6

Ingredients

1 pound hot breakfast sausage

½ bag (15 oz) frozen hash browns, shredded

1 cups cheddar cheese, shredded

4 eggs

1 cup milk

¼ teaspoon pepper

¼ teaspoon garlic powder

¼ teaspoon onion powder

- ½ teaspoon salt

Directions

In the large skillet cook sausages until no longer pink. Drain fat.

Add shredded hash browns to the skillet and cook until lightly brown.

Place hash browns in the bottom of oven proof pan, lightly greased. Top with sausages and cheese.

It the bowl whisk together eggs, salt, pepper, garlic powder, onion powder, and milk.

Pour egg mixture over the hash browns.

1. **Preheat the Air Fryer to 350-370 F**

Place the pan in the fryer into the fryer and cook for 25-30 minutes, until become ready.

Delicious English Breakfast

Prep time: 5 minutes

Cook time: 13-15 minutes

Servings: 4

Ingredients

8 chestnut mushrooms

8 tomatoes

4 eggs

1 clove garlic, halved

4 slices smoked bacon, crushed

4 chipolatas

7 oz baby leaf spinach

1 tablespoon extra virgin olive oil

- Salt and ground black pepper to taste

Directions

Preheat the Air fryer to 390 F

Place the mushrooms, tomatoes, and garlic in a round tin. Season with salt and ground pepper and spray with olive oil. Place the tin, bacon, and chipolatas in the cooking basket of your Air Fryer. Cook for 10 minutes.

Meanwhile, wilt the spinach in a microwave or by pouring boiling water through it in a sieve. Drain well.

Add the spinach to the tin and crack in the eggs. Reduce the temperature to 300 F and cook for couple minutes more, until the eggs are prepared.

1. Sprinkle with freshly chopped herbs you prefer and serve.

Healthy Breakfast

Prep time: 5 minutes

Cook time: 10 minutes

Servings: 2

Ingredients

4 large eggs

1 teaspoon mustard

2 tablespoon mayonnaise

2 tablespoon chopped green onion

½ teaspoon smoked paprika

- A pinch of salt and black pepper

Directions

Mix together eggs, mustard, mayo, and chopped green onion.

Season with salt, pepper, and paprika.

Pour the mixture in the baking tray which fits to your air fryer.

1. Cook for 10 minutes at 370 F.

Breakfast Sandwich

Prep time: 5 minutes

Cook time: 7 minutes

Servings: 1

Ingredients

1 egg, beaten

2 streaky bacon stripes

1 English muffin

- A pinch of salt and pepper

Directions

Beat 1 egg into an oven proof cup or bowl.

Preheat the Air fryer to 390°F

Place the egg in the cup, bacon stripes and muffin to the fryer and cook for 6-7 minutes.

1. Get the sandwich together and enjoy.

Mac & Cheese with Topping

Prep time: 20 minutes

Cook time: 5 minutes

Servings: 3-4

Ingredients

3 cups macaroni

15 pcs Ritz biscuits

2 oz gruyere cheese, grated

2 oz butter

2 tablespoon plain flour

16 oz milk

1 clove garlic, minced

- 1 cup pizza cheese mix (Mozzarella, Parmesan, Cheddar)

Directions

Crush Ritz biscuits, mix with gruyere cheese and set aside.

Cook macaroni until almost ready, drained and also set aside.

Melt the butter in the separate bowl on the small fire and fry the garlic until fragrant. Add plain flour. Add milk and stir until mixture thickens and looks like a creamy soup. Add remained gruyere cheese and let it melt in the sauce.

Bring this sauce to a simmer and switch off the fire. Add macaroni into the mixture and combine well.

Dish into individual ceramic bowls.

1. **Spoon with Ritz biscuits mixture over macaroni. Top with pizza cheese mix.**
2. **Preheat the air fryer to 350 F**
3. Place ceramic bowls into the Air Fryer and cook for 5 minutes or until pizza cheese mix becomes golden.

Toasts with Cheese

Prep time: 10 minutes

Cook time: 6 minutes

Servings: 2

Ingredients

2 sliced white bread

4 oz cheese, grated

- Little piece of butter

Directions

At first, toast the bread in the toaster.

Once toasted, spread the butter on bread pieces.

Cover with grated cheese.

Preheat the Air Fryer to 350 F

1. Place covered bread slices into the fryer and cook for 4-6 minutes.

Baked Eggs in Avocado Nests

Prep time: 5 minutes

Cook time: 20 minutes

Servings: 2

Ingredients

1 large avocado, halved

2 eggs

4 grape tomato, halved

2 teaspoon chives, chopped

- A pinch of sea salt and black pepper

Directions

Cut avocado in half length-wise. Remove the pit and widen the hole in each half by scraping out the avocado flesh with the help of the spoon.

Place avocado halves in a small oven proof baking dish cut side up.

Beat an egg into each half of avocado. Season with salt and pepper.

Cook for about 10-15 minutes in 370°F into the Air Fryer.

1. Top with grape tomato halves and chives. Enjoy!

Fried Eggs with Ham

Prep time: 5 minutes

Cook time: 10-15 minutes

Servings: 4

Ingredients

4 large eggs

2 oz (nearly 2 thin slices) ham

2 teaspoon butter

2 tablespoon heavy cream

3 tablespoon parmesan cheese, grated

2 teaspoon fresh chives, chopped

A pinch of smoked paprika

- Salt and ground black pepper to taste

Directions

Grease the pie pan with butter and line the bottom with ham slices. Make the bottom and sides of the pie pan completely covered with ham.

In a small bowl beat 1 egg, add heavy cream, a pinch of salt and 1/8 teaspoon ground pepper. Whisk to combine.

Pour this egg mixture over the ham and beat remaining 3 eggs over top.

Season with salt and ground pepper, sprinkle with parmesan cheese.

Preheat the Air Fryer to 320-350 F

1. **Place the pie pan into the cooking basket and cook for 12 minutes.**

When finished, remove fried eggs from the pie pan with the help of spatula and transfer to the plate. Season with smoked paprika and chopped chives.

Sandwich with Prosciutto, Tomato and Herbs

Prep time: 2-3 minutes

Cook time: 5 minutes

Servings: 2

Ingredients

2 slices bread

2 slices prosciutto

2 slices tomato

2 slices mozzarella cheese

2 basil leaves

1 teaspoon olive oil

- Salt and black pepper for seasoning

Directions

Take 2 pieces of bread. Add prosciutto on the top. Add mozzarella cheese.

Place the sandwich into the Air Fryer and cook for 5 minutes in 380°F without preheating.

Using a spatula remove the sandwich.

1. Drizzle olive oil on top. Season with salt and pepper, add tomato and basil.

French Toast Sticks

Prep time: 5 minutes

Cook time: 5-8 minutes

Servings: 2

Ingredients

4 pieces bread, sliced

2 tablespoon soft butter

2 eggs, beaten

¼ teaspoon cinnamon

¼ teaspoon nutmeg

¼ teaspoon ground cloves

Icing sugar for garnish

- A pinch of salt

Directions

It the bowl beat two eggs, sprinkle with salt, cinnamon, nutmeg and ground cloves.

Butter both sides of bread and cut into stripes.

Preheat the Air Fryer to 350-370 F

Dip each bread strip into the egg mixture and then put into the air fryer.

Cook for about 5-8 minutes until eggs are cooked and bread become golden.

Garnish with icing sugar and top with cream or maple syrup (as for your desire).

Cheese Omelet

PREP TIME: 8-12 MINUTES

COOKING TIME: 13 MINUTES

SERVES: 1

175ºC FRY

Cooking spray

1 diced onion

3 eggs

3 mL soy sauce

11 grams grated cheddar cheese

Salt to taste

Black pepper to taste

(Optional) salsa

In a small bowl, whisk the eggs and soy sauce with salt and pepper.

Coat the small pan with cooking spray.

Spread the diced onion on the bottom of the pan and put the pan in the fryer.

Air fry until onions are translucent. It should take 5-8 minutes.

Pull out the pan and pour in the egg mixture. Spread the shredded cheddar on top.

Cook for another 5 minutes.

Pull out the pan to see if the eggs are set. If not, cook for another 2 minutes.

Serve omelet with a dollop of salsa and toast (optional).

Dutch Oven Baked French Toast with Eggs

PREP TIME: 8-12 MINUTES

COOKING TIME: 10 MINUTES

SERVES: 1-2

160°C FRY

Cooking spray

2 slices multigrain bread

2 eggs

150 grams chopped or ground sausage

2 mL balsamic vinegar

2 mL maple syrup

A pinch Italian seasoning

16 grams cheddar cheese

4-6 slices tomatoes

Salt to taste

Black pepper to taste

Mayonnaise to serve

Use cooking spray to coat either the baking dish or the baking accessory.

Preheat the air fryer.

Lay the slices of bread inside the dish and scatter the sausage on top of the bread.

Lay the tomato slices on top of the sausage and sprinkle the cheese on top.

You can either beat the eggs before pouring over the other ingredients or break whole eggs and pour them directly over the other ingredients.

Pour the maple syrup and vinegar over everything, then scatter the sausage on top. Salt and pepper to taste.

Put the dish inside the basket and the basket inside the air fryer.

Bake for 10 minutes, then remove from fryer.

Serve with mayonnaise

Shimeji Mushroom Omelet
PREP TIME: 8-12 MINUTES

COOKING TIME: 25 MINUTES

SERVES: 1

175ºC FRY

75 grams fresh sliced Shimeji mushrooms

100 grams sliced silken tofu

2 eggs

1 minced garlic clove

20 grams diced onion

Salt to taste

Black pepper to taste

Cooking spray

Use cooking spray to coat the baking accessory.

Preheat the air fryer.

Place garlic and onions inside the air fryer and cook for 4 minutes.

Pull it out and add mushrooms and tofu to the garlic and onions.

In a small bowl, whisk salt and pepper into the eggs.

Pour this mixture over the vegetables and tofu.

Put back in the air fryer and cook for 20-25 minutes. Use a toothpick to check if the eggs are cooked through.

French Toast Sticks

PREP TIME: 5 MINUTES / COOKING TIME: 7MINUTES / SERVES 2

175ºC FRY

Cooking spray

4 beaten eggs

8 slices multigrain bread

Salt to taste

A pinch ground nutmeg

A pinch cinnamon

A pinch ground cloves

60 grams softened butter

Maple syrup, on the side

Whist eggs and spices together.

Spread butter on both sides of each bread slice, then cut bread into strips 1-inch wide.

Preheat the air fryer.

As you would when making French toast, soak the bread in the egg.

Lay the eggy bread strips in the pan inside the air fryer. Cook for 7 minutes. If the strips do not all fit without overlapping, then cook them in batches.

Partway through cooking, pull out the pan, spray the bread strips with cooking spray, flip, and spray the other side. Then put the pan back and finish cooking.

The French toast should be a golden-brown color when done. Serve with maple syrup.

Button Mushrooms with Parmesan
PREP TIME: 15 MINUTES

COOKING TIME: 7 MINUTES

SERVES: 1-2

175ºC FRY

45 grams grated Parmesan cheese

450 grams button mushrooms

30 grams whole wheat bread crumbs

15 grams whole wheat flour

1 large egg

Salt to taste

Black pepper to taste

Marinara for dipping

Combine the parmesan and bread crumbs in a small bowl.

Preheat the air fryer.

On a separate plate, dredge the mushrooms in flour.

Once coated with flour, dip mushrooms into the egg, then into the breadcrumb and cheese mixture.

Put coated mushrooms in the basket of the air fryer.

Cook mushrooms in small batches for 6-8 minutes, occasionally flipping them. Mushrooms should be golden colored when done.

Serve on a platter with a bowl of marinara for dipping.

Frittata with Sausage and Parmesan
PREP TIME: 8-12 MINUTES

COOKING TIME: 10 MINUTES

SERVES: 4

175ºC BAKE

6 eggs

8 halved cherry tomatoes

11 grams shredded Parmesan cheese

1 chopped Italian sausage

30 mL olive oil

Salt to taste

Black pepper to taste

Preheat the air fryer

Put the sausage and tomatoes inside the baking dish or baking accessory. Place the dish inside the fryer and bake for 5 minutes.

In a medium sized bowl, whisk together eggs, oil, salt, pepper and cheese.

Pull out the baking dish and spread the egg mixture on top of the sausage and tomatoes.

Replace the dish in the fryer. Cook for an additional 5 minutes.

Serve hot.

Red Pepper Soufflé
PREP TIME: 8-12 MINUTES

COOKING TIME: 8 MINUTES

SERVES: 2

175ºC BAKE

4 beaten eggs

60 mL light cream

20 grams fresh minced parsley

1 small diced red bell pepper

Salt to taste

Black pepper to taste

Whisk all ingredients together in a medium-sized bowl.

Preheat the air fryer.

Pour into ramekins, filling only halfway.

Put the ramekins inside the air fryer basket. Put the basket inside the fryer.

Bake for 5-8 minutes, then pull them out of the fryer.

Serve immediately.

European Breakfast
PREP TIME: 6-8 MINUTES

COOKING TIME: 20 MINUTES

SERVES 2

160ºC, 200ºC BAKE

4 sausages

2 eggs

4 un-smoked pork loin

½ can baked beans

4 slice toasted multigrain bread

Preheat the air fryer to 160° C.

Put the pork loin and sausages in the fryer and cook for 10 minutes.

Get 3 ramekins. Pour the baked beans into one and crack each egg into a ramekin.

Set the temperature at 200° C. Put the ramekins in the fryer with the sausages and cook for 10 minutes.

Pull out the ramekins and sausages from the fryer.

Serve on a platter with toasted multigrain bread.

Creamy Mushrooms

PREP TIME: 15 MINUTES

COOKING TIME: 10 MINUTES

SERVES: 2

180°C FRY

1 dozen chopped mushrooms

1 strip chopped bacon

20 grams diced green bell pepper

20 grams chopped carrots

20 grams diced onions

45 grams grated cheese of your choice, + extra cheese to top

60 mL sour cream

Set aside the sour cream and grated cheese. Place the other ingredients in a pan and sauté over medium heat until the vegetables are soft.

Preheat the air fryer to 180 degrees C.

Transfer the vegetables into the baking accessory. Mix in the sour cream and grated cheese.

If you want to, sprinkle more cheese on top.

Put the baking accessory into the basket and put the basket in the air fryer.

Air fry for 10 minutes, then serve hot.

Savory Oatmeal with Beans and Peppers
PREP TIME: 8-12 MINUTES

COOKING TIME: 7 MINUTES

SERVES: 2-3

180°C FRY

20 grams cooked chickpeas

20 grams cooked kidney beans

2 large bell peppers, cut in half lengthwise

400 grams cooked oatmeal

A pinch paprika

2 grams ground cumin

Salt to taste

Black pepper to taste

120 mL plain yogurt

Preheat the air fryer.

Lay the peppers face down in the air fryer and cook for 3 minutes.

Pull out the peppers and set them aside.

In a small bowl, combine the remaining ingredients.

Fill the bell pepper halves with the oatmeal and bean mixture.

Put the pepper halves back in the air fryer and cook for an additional 4 minutes.

Serve with yogurt to top.

Spiced Toast

PREP TIME: 5-7 MINUTES

COOKING TIME: 4 MINUTES

SERVES: 2-3

200°C FRY

6 slices multigrain bread

60 grams chickpea flour

1 diced medium onion

1 sliced green chili

Water as required

10 grams fresh diced cilantro

A pinch chili powder

Salt to taste

Oil as needed

Pour the chickpea flour in a large bowl and add water, 15 mL at a time, until the batter is cohesive and easy to drip or spread.

Mix in the remaining ingredients except for the slices of bread.

Line the air fryer basket with aluminum foil.

Spread the batter on both sides of each slice of bread, then lay the bread slices in the air fryer basket.

Cook for a total of 4 minutes. If necessary, cook in batches.

After 2 minutes, either use cooking spray or use a pastry brush to apply a small amount of oil to the bread slices.

Serve with the condiment or dip of your choice.

Ham and Egg Croissants
PREP TIME: 8-12 MINUTES

COOKING TIME: 8 MINUTES

SERVES: 2

160°C BAKE

2 eggs

8 chopped button mushrooms

6 shaved slices honey ham

8 halved cherry tomatoes

45 grams cheddar cheese

Optional: 1 sprig minced rosemary

Salt to taste

Black pepper to taste

A dab of melted butter

2 croissants

Salad greens to serve

Use the melted butter to grease a small baking dish or the baking accessory.

Preheat the air fryer.

Place all ingredients in layers inside the air fryer except for the croissants and salad greens.

Make 2 depressions in the ham layer. Crack an egg into each of the depressions.

Top with a layer of cheese and season with rosemary, salt and pepper.

Place the croissants on top and carefully ease the baking dish inside the basket of the air fryer.

Bake for a total of 8 minutes.

Pull the croissants out after 4 minutes, or less if you prefer croissants less toasted.

Serve as a sandwich with the baked ham and egg on top of the croissant halves and salad greens on the side.

Bacon and Egg Breakfast Sandwich

PREP TIME: 2-4 MINUTES

COOKING TIME: 6 MINUTES

SERVES: 2

200ºC BAKE

2 eggs

2 strips English bacon

2 English muffins

Salt to taste

Black pepper to taste

Preheat the air fryer.

Gather 2 ovenproof cups, or ramekins, and crack an egg into each. Season with salt and black pepper.

Put the ramekins, along with the English muffins and bacon, inside the air fryer.

Cook for a total of 6 minutes.

2 minutes in, pull out the English muffins.

Slice the English muffins and make a sandwich with the bacon and eggs when they're done cooking.

Serve hot.

Parmesan Toast

PREP TIME: 6-8 MINUTES

COOKING TIME: 5 MINUTES

SERVES: 2

200ºC BAKE

4 slices multigrain bread

60 mL butter

60 mL Branston pickle

22 grams shredded Parmesan

Preheat the air fryer.

Spread 15 mL of butter on each slice of multigrain bread.

Spread 15 mL of Branston pickle on top of the butter.

Scatter the Parmesan across the bread slices.

Wrap the bottom of the air fryer basket with aluminum foil.

Lay the slices of bread on the bottom of the basket. Cook for 5 minutes.

Serve immediately

Appetizer

Feta Pastries
PREP TIME: 30-40 MINUTES

COOKING TIME: 3 MINUTES

SERVES: 10-14

200°C BAKE

10 filo pastry sheets

90 grams crumbled feta cheese

2 diced green onions

16 grams chopped parsley

Freshly ground black pepper

Salt to taste

Olive oil as needed

In a small bowl combine parsley, green onion, feta, salt and pepper.

Divide each pastry sheet equally into 3 pieces.

Place a small amount of the feta filling on a piece of filo pastry and fold the filo over the feta mixture to make a triangle shape. Continue folding the pastry over the filling, maintaining the triangle shape, until the piece of filo is used up. Use a dab of water to seal the final flap of filo. Each strip of filo will make a single triangle, resulting in 30 triangles total.

Preheat the air fryer.

Once you are done forming the triangles, brush them with a small amount of oil.

Bake 5 triangles at a time in the air fryer basket for 3 minutes each. They should be golden brown when done.

Serve hot with a dip on the side.

Mushroom and Onion Croquettes

PREP TIME: 2 1/2 HOURS

COOKING TIME: 8 MINUTES

SERVES: 3-4

200°C FRY

10 chopped mushrooms

1 medium chopped onion

30 mL butter

30 mL vegetable oil

A pinch ground nutmeg

475 mL unsweetened almond milk

22 grams flour

75 grams breadcrumbs

Salt to taste

Black pepper to taste

Melt the butter in a skillet over medium heat, then add onions and mushrooms. Sauté briefly, then add the flour and continue to sauté.

Stir the milk into the skillet and cook until the mixture thickens. Mix in the nutmeg, salt and pepper.

Let the mixture in the skillet cool completely then transfer it to the refrigerator for 2 hours.

In a medium-sized bowl, combine the vegetable oil and breadcrumbs until crumbly and not overly sticky.

Pull the onions and mushroom mixture out of the fridge and shape into balls.

Preheat the air fryer to 200 degrees C.

Roll the balls in breadcrumbs then transfer them to the air fryer basket.

Air fry for 8 minutes.

Serve warm with dip of your choice.

Cheesy Potato Balls

PREP TIME: 14-16 MINUTES

COOKING TIME: 10 MINUTES

SERVES: 4

200ºC FRY

4 medium potatoes

120 mL fresh mozzarella cheese, cut into bite-sized chunks.

2 slices multigrain bread

A pinch black pepper

Chili powder to taste

A pinch cumin powder

Salt to taste

Cornstarch, to dust

Peel the potatoes. Put them in a saucepan on the stove and boil them. Once soft, mash potatoes.

Briefly run the slices of bread under water. Press out any excess water. Add the slices of bread to the mashed potatoes.

Mix in the remaining ingredients except for the cornstarch and mozzarella.

Preheat the air fryer.

Shape the mashed potato mixture around the chunks of mozzarella. This should make about 7 balls.

Dredge the mozzarella and mashed potato balls in cornstarch. Transfer them to the fryer basket.

Air fry for 10 minutes.

Fried Fish Fillets

PREP TIME: 14-16 MINUTES

COOKING TIME: 12 MINUTES

SERVES: 8

180°C FRY

8 fish fillets

2 eggs

8 grams minced garlic

80 mL olive oil

150 grams breadcrumbs

Lemon wedges to serve

In a medium sized bowl, combine olive oil, breadcrumbs, and garlic.

Whisk eggs.

Preheat the air fryer.

Dip the fish fillets in the egg, then dredge them in breadcrumbs. Put the fillets in the air fryer basket.

Air fry the fish fillets for 10-12 minutes.

Serve immediately with lemon wedges on the side.

Vegetable Pakora

PREP TIME: 18-22 MINUTES

COOKING TIME: 10 MINUTES

SERVES: 4-5

200ºC FRY

1 large chopped onion

1 small head cauliflower, chopped into bite-size pieces

150 grams chopped spinach

1 large peeled potato, chopped into bite-size pieces

1 chopped green chili

A pinch chili powder

3 grams garlic paste/powder

3 grams ground cumin

120 grams chickpea or garbanzo flour

Salt to taste

Cooking spray

Combine all ingredients except for the flour. Set aside to allow water to drain from the vegetables.

Mix in flour. Add extra water if necessary to create a thick mixture that can be dropped by the spoonful.

Preheat air fryer.

Wrap the air fryer basket with aluminum foil. Drop the fritters into the basket. Use cooking spray on the fritters.

Air fry fritters for 10 minutes.

Serve hot with the condiment of your choice.

Potato and Parmesan Croquettes

PREP TIME: 10-12 MINUTES

COOKING TIME: 8 MINUTES

SERVES: 3-4

200°C FRY

1 large potato

7 grams flour

A pinch ground nutmeg

10 grams fresh chopped chives

11 grams grated Parmesan cheese

Salt to taste

Black pepper to taste

For coating:

40 grams breadcrumbs

15 mL vegetable oil

Peel, boil and mash the potato.

In a large bowl, combine all ingredients, including the mashed potato.

Preheat the air fryer.

Shape the mixture into balls.

In a small, separate bowl, combine breadcrumbs and vegetable oil.

Dredge the balls in the breadcrumb mixture then transfer to the air fryer basket.

Air fry for 8 minutes.

Serve with condiment of your choice.

Savory Stuffed Mushrooms with Parmesan

PREP TIME: 16 MINUTES

COOKING TIME: 8 MINUTES

SERVES: 3-4

180°C FRY

1 rasher bacon

1 dozen medium sized mushrooms, stems diced and set aside

1 small diced carrot

20 grams diced green bell pepper

1 small diced onion

60 mL sour cream

45 grams Parmesan cheese, plus extra for sprinkling

In a skillet over medium heat, sauté bacon, bell pepper, onion, mushrooms, and carrot until soft.

Mix in the parmesan cheese and sour cream.

Stuff the mushrooms with the vegetable mixture.

Preheat the air fryer.

Place the stuffed mushrooms in the air fryer basket and scatter additional parmesan on them, if desired.

Air fry mushrooms for 8 minutes.

Serve on a platter with a dip of your choice.

Ricotta Bites
PREP TIME: 14-16 MINUTES

COOKING TIME: 8 MINUTES

SERVES: 7-10

200°C

2 eggs

475 mL grated ricotta

20 grams diced chives

30 grams whole wheat flour

20 grams fresh diced basil

3 grams orange zest

Salt to taste

Black pepper to taste

For coating:

40 grams whole wheat breadcrumbs

15 mL vegetable oil

Separate the egg yolks and whites.

In a medium-sized bowl, combine the flour, egg yolks, orange zest, chives, salt and pepper. Use your hands to mix in the ricotta.

Form balls with the ricotta mixture.

In a separate bowl, mix the breadcrumbs and vegetable oil together.

Preheat the air fryer.

Dredge the ricotta balls in the breadcrumbs then transfer them to the air fryer basket.

Air fry for 8 minutes.

Serve with the condiment of your choice.

Green Beans with Shallots and Almonds

Prep time: 5 minutes | cook time: 25 minutes | servings: 4-5

Ingredients

1½ pound French green beans, stems removed

½ pound shallots, peeled, stems removed and cut into quarters

¼ cup slivered almonds, lightly roasted

2 tablespoon olive oil

1 tablespoon salt

- ½ teaspoon black pepper, ground

Directions

Bring water to a boil over high heat. Once boiling, add the green beans, season with salt and cook for 2 minutes. Remove from the water and drain in a colander.

Mix cooked beans with quartered shallots, some additional salt and black pepper and sprinkle with the olive oil. Toss well to coat evenly.

Cook bean mixture for 25 minutes at 390 F tossing them twice throughout the cooking process. The green beans should be lightly browned and tender once cooked.

1. Transfer cooked beans to a serving platter.
2.

Pizza with Pepperoni

Prep time: 5 minutes | cook time: 5 minutes | servings: 3

Ingredients

3 cleaned and scooped portabella mushroom caps

3 tablespoons tomato sauce

3 tablespoons olive oil

3 tablespoons shredded mozzarella

12 slices pepperoni

1 pinch dried Italian seasoning

- 1 pinches salt

Directions

In the air fryer heated on 330°F put olive oil and drizzle both sides of mushrooms. Add Italian season and salt, spread with tomato sauce and put the cheese on the top.

After a minute put the pepperoni on the top of the pizza (do that outside of the fryer!) and cook for 3-5 minutes.

At the end, frost with the parmesan on the top.

Feta Pillows

Prep time: 10 minutes | cook time: 10 minutes | servings: 4

Ingredients

1 egg yolk

2 tablespoons flat-leafed parsley

4 ounces feta cheese

1 finely chopped scallion

2 finely chopped sheets of frozen filo pastry, but now defrosted

2 tablespoons olive oil

- Ground black pepper to taste

Directions

Mix beat egg yolk with feta, scallion, parsley and pepper in a bowl.

Each sheet of filo cut into three strips.

This pasta put with a spoon in the strip of pastry and make a pillow or triangle.

1. Cook in air fryer at 390 F for 3 minutes and then cook on 360 F for 2 minutes.
2.

Classic Spring Rolls

Prep time: 5 minutes | cook time: 15 minutes, servings: 4

Ingredients for Rolls

1 beaten egg

8 spring rolls wrappers

1 teaspoon cornstarch

- ¼ teaspoon vegetable oil

Ingredients for Stuffing

4 oz. cooked and shredded chicken breast

1 sliced thin carrot, medium size

1 sliced thin celery stalk

1 teaspoon sugar

½ cup sliced thin mushrooms

½ teaspoon finely chopped ginger

- 1 teaspoon chicken stock powder

Directions

First, you need to make the filling. Chicken put into a bowl and mix with the carrot, celery, and mushrooms. After that, put ginger, chicken stock powder and sugar and stir.

Egg put with cornstarch and mix until it's made paste

Now, put filling on roll wrapper, roll it and close with egg.

1. Put rolls brushed with oil into air fryer on 390°F and cook for 3-4 minutes. Serve with soy or chili sauce.
2.

Delicious Breaded Mushrooms

Prep time: 10 minutes | cook time: 7-10 minutes | servings: 3

Ingredients

10 oz button mushrooms

¼ cup flour

1 egg

½ cup breadcrumbs

3 oz cheese, finely grated

- Salt and pepper for seasoning

Directions

In the middle bowl mix breadcrumbs with cheese, season with salt and pepper to taste and set aside.

In another middle bowl beat an egg and also set aside.

Wash and dry mushrooms with the paper towels.

Preheat the air fryer to 340-360°F

Roll mushrooms in the flour, dip them into the beaten egg and dip in the breadcrumbs and cheese mixture.

Place to the fryer and cook for 7-10 minutes. Shake once while cooking.

Serve warm with any sauce you like.

Crunchy Jalapeno Peppers

Prep time: 20 minutes | cook time: 10 minutes | servings: 2

Ingredients

2-3 jalapeno peppers, sliced

1 oz cheddar cheese

1 spring roll wrapper

- 1 tablespoon Egg Beaters

Directions

Trim stem end off, core and slice lengthwise.

Cut cheese into ½ oz strips.

Peel off a sheet of spring roll wrapper and cut in half. Cover each half with a half tablespoon of liquid egg mixture.

Place a half of jalapeno pepper in one corner of the spring roll wrapper half (egg-brushed side up), then place a strip of cheese and then another half of jalapeno.

Roll the pepper and cheese tightly in the spring roll wrapper on the diagonal.

Check all sides and glue any loose edges with egg mixture.

Preheat the air fryer to 370 F

Lightly spray each wrapping with cooking spray and put them into the air fryer. Cook for about 10 minutes until they become brown.

Baked Cheesy Crescents

Prep time: 15 minutes | cook time: 15 minutes | servings: 4-5

Ingredients

1 pound ground beef

8 oz cream cheese softened

2 cans crescent rolls

- Salt and pepper to taste

Directions

In the skillet prepare ground beef until becomes ready. Drain fat.

In the bowl mix cooked ground beef and cream cheese. Season the mixture with salt and pepper to taste.

Separate rolls into triangles. Cut each triangle in half length-wise.

Scoop a heaping tablespoon into each roll and roll up.

Preheat the air fryer into 370 F

Bake for 15 minutes until crescents become golden and ready.

Roasted Pepper Rolls with Feta

Prep time: 10 minutes | cook time 10 minutes | servings: 3

Ingredients

2-3 medium-sized yellow or red peppers, halved

4 oz Greek feta cheese, crushed

1 green onion, sliced

- 2 tablespoon oregano, chopped

Directions

Preheat the air fryer to 380°F

Place peppers in the cooking basket and turn on the fryer.

Roast peppers for 10 minutes until skin will become slightly charred.

Halve peppers longways and remove skin and seeds.

Prepare filling: combine Greek feta cheese with green onion and oregano.

Coat pepper pieces with feta mixture and roll them up, starting from the narrowest end.

Fix the rolls with tapas forks and serve.

Rice and Vegetable Stuffed Tomatoes

Prep time: 12 minutes | cook time 25 minutes | servings: 4

Ingredients

3 tomatoes, cored

2 cups white rice, cooked

1 medium onion, diced

1 medium carrot, diced

1 tablespoon Olive oil

1 clove garlic, minced

Ground pepper

- Salt

Directions

Sprinkle the olive oil in a skillet and sauté carrot, onion, and garlic for 2-3 minutes, season the mixture with salt and pepper.

Add cooked rice to the vegetable mixture, stir to combine.

Preheat the air fryer to 340°F.

Fill in cored tomatoes with mixture.

Place stuffed tomatoes into the air fryer and cook for 20-25 minutes.

Serve warm and enjoy.

Broccoli with Cheddar cheese

Prep time: 10 minutes | cook time: 12 minutes | servings: 3-4

Ingredients

1 head broccoli, steamed and chopped

1 tablespoon olive oil

1 ½ cup Cheddar cheese, grated

- 1 teaspoon salt

Preparation

Steam the broccoli, cool after that and separate pieces from the stem.

In a large bowl combine broccoli florets with grated cheddar cheese.

Preheat the air fryer to 340-360°F.

Place broccoli and cheese mixture to the blender, pulse couple times.

Form balls from the mixture with your hands, about 0,5-1 inch in diameter.

Place broccoli balls into the Fryer sprinkle with oil and cook for 10-12 minutes.

Remove the balls, sprinkle with salt and serve with sour cream, or any sauce you like.

Asparagus Spears Rolled with Bacon

Prep time: 10 minutes | cook time: 9 minutes | servings: 4

Ingredients

1 bundle asparagus, 20-25 spears

4 slices bacon

1 garlic clove, crushed

½ tablespoon olive oil

½ tablespoon sesame oil

1 ½ tablespoon brown sugar

- ½ tablespoon toasted sesame seeds

Directions

In a medium bowl combine oils, brown sugar, and crushed garlic.

Separate bundle of asparagus into four equal-sized bunches and wrap each in a bacon slice.

Cover asparagus bunches with oil mixture.

Preheat the air fryer to 340-360°F

Put bunches into the Fryer and sprinkle with sesame seeds.

Cook for approximately 8 minutes.

Serve and enjoy.

Mushrooms Stuffed with Garlic

Prep time: 10 minutes | cook time: 10 minutes | servings: 4

Ingredients

- 16 small pieces of mushrooms

For Stuffing

1 ½ slices of white bread

1 tablespoon finely chopped flat-leafed parsley

1 crushed garlic clove

1 ½ tablespoon olive oil

- Ground black pepper to taste

Directions

Mix all ingredients in a food processor and stir with olive oil.

Mushrooms cut and separate from stalks and the caps fill with the breadcrumbs and other ingredients.

Cook for 7-8 minutes on 390°F.

1. Season with black pepper to taste

Appetizing Fried Cheese

Prep time: 15 minutes | cook time 15 minutes | servings: 2

Ingredients

4 slices of white bread or brioche if you have one

¼ cup melted butter

- ½ cup sharp cheddar cheese

Directions

Cheese and butter put in two bowls. On the each side of the bread brush the butter, and on two of sides put cheese.

Grilled cheese put together with bread and all put in air fryer at 360°F for 5-7 minutes.

Stuffed Mushroom Caps

Prep time: 10 minutes | cook time: 5 minutes | servings: 3

Ingredients

10 mushrooms

4 bacon slices, cut

¼ middle onion, diced

½ cup cheese, grated

- Ground black pepper and salt, to taste

Directions

Wash mushrooms, drain well and remove stems.

Combine bacon, cut into ½ inch pieces, diced onion and grated cheese.

Season mushroom caps with salt and pepper.

Put bacon mixture to the seasoned mushroom caps.

Preheat the air fryer to 380 F

Place mushrooms into the air fryer and cook for 5 minutes until cheese melted.

Serve and enjoy.

Melt-in-Mouth Salmon Quiche with Broccoli

Prep time: 10 minutes, cook time: 20 minutes, servings: 3-4

Ingredients

1/3 pound salmon fillet, cut into 1/2-inch pieces

1/2 cup all-purpose flour

1/4 cup cold butter

3 tablespoon whipping cream

2 large eggs

1 egg yolk

2 teaspoon freshly squeezed lemon juice

1 green onion, sliced

½ cup broccoli florets

- Salt and ground black pepper to taste

Directions

Preheat the air fryer to 380 F.

In the mixing bowl combine salmon fillets, salt, ground pepper and lemon juice. Set aside the mixture for 5-10 minutes.

In another bowl mix the butter with the egg yolk and flour. Add a tablespoon of cold water and then roll the mixture into a ball.

Roll the dough out on a floured surface as needed.

Place the batter into the quiche pan and press on edges. Trim the edges.

In the large bowl combine the eggs and whipping cream. Add some salt and pepper to taste.

Pour the mixture over the dough in the quiche pan and transfer salmon cubes along with the sliced onions and broccoli florets.

Place the pan in the air fryer basket and cook for 20 minutes.

When ready, top the quiche with extra green onions and serve hot.

You can also serve it cold or microwave it if desired.

Mini-pigs in Blankets

Prep time: 10 minutes | cook time: 10 minutes | servings: 3

Ingredients

1 tin (8 oz) mini frankfurters

4 oz puff pastry

- 1 tablespoon smooth mustard plus some more for serving

Directions

Dry frankfurters with paper towels.

Cut the puff pastry into 2x1-inch strips.

Spread the stripes with mustard.

Preheat the air fryer to 370°F

Wrap each sausage with pastry stripes.

Put them into the fryer and cook for nearly 10 minutes or until they will become golden

Serve with mustard for dipping.

Spicy Grilled Tomatoes

Prep time: 5 minutes | cook time: 20 minutes | servings: 2

Ingredients

2 large tomatoes, sliced

Herb mix (parsley, oregano, basil, thyme, rosemary or something else)

Ground pepper and salt to taste

- 1 tablespoon olive oil or cooking spray

Directions

Cut tomatoes in half. Turn halves cut side up. Sprinkle tops with olive oil or cooking spray. Season with ground pepper and herbs dried or fresh.

Cook tomato halves in the air fryer for 20 minutes at 330 F.

Cheeseburger

Prep time: 10 minutes | cook time: 5 minutes | servings: 3

Ingredients

1 pound ground beef

6 dinner rolls

6 slices cheddar cheese

- Salt and pepper to taste

Directions

As you expect, first you need to from the burgers from beef. The perfect is into 6 2.5-ounce patties. Put salt and pepper as you like, but not too much.

Put in air fryer (which you preheated to 390°F) burgers and cook for 10 minutes, then remove from the fryer, put the cheese on it and back into the fryer for one minute more. That's it.

Now you can enjoy in perfect burgers without fat.

Lunch Recipes

Since air fryers are quick, they make the perfect way to prepare any lunch. You'll find that these lunch recipes are both tasty and quick.

Tuna English Muffin Sandwich
Prep Time: 8-10 Minutes

Cook Time: 5 Minutes

Ingredients:

6 Ounces Tuna, Chunk Light & Drained

¼ Cup Mayonnaise

2 Tablespoons Mustard

1 Tablespoon Lemon Juice

2 Green Onions, Minced

3 Tablespoons Butter, Softened

6 Slices Provolone, Thin

- 3 English Muffins, Split

Directions:

Preheat to 390 degrees.

Take your tuna, mayonnaise, lemon juice, green onions and mustard, mixing them all in a small bowl.

Butter the cut sides of your English muffin, and put them in your air fryer with the butter side up. Cook for two to four minutes or until the English muffins are golden brown. Remove them from your air fryer.

Place a slice of cheese on each side of your muffin, and grill in your air fryer for another two to four minutes. The cheese should melt and start to brown.

1. Remove them from the air fryer and top with your tuna mixture.

Mushroom Cordon Bleu

Prep Time: 5-10 Minutes

Cooking Time: 10 Minutes

Ingredients:

1 Medium Egg, Beaten

2 Cups Chickpea Flour

4 Portabella Mushroom Caps

2 Cups Cream Cheese

1 Tablespoon Garlic Powder

1 Large Egg

1 Tablespoon Onion Powder

1 Cup Mozzarella Cheese, Shredded

- 4 Slices Ham

Directions:

Start by heating your air fryer to 390 degrees.

Take one of your eggs, garlic powder, cream cheese and onion powder and mix it in a bowl. Spread this mixture onto your mushroom caps.

Top it with ham and mozzarella cheese.

Dip each mushroom in egg, and then dip it in the chickpea flour.

1. Place it in your air fryer and let it cook for ten minutes.

Zucchini & Tuna Melts

Prep Time: 15 Minutes

Cooking Time: 10 Minutes

Ingredients:

4 Corn Tortillas

3 Tablespoons Butter, Softened

6 Ounces Chunk Light Tuna, Drained

1 Cup Zucchini, Shredded & Drained

1/3 Cup Mayonnaise

2 Tablespoons Mustard

- 1 Cup Cheddar Cheese, Shredded

Directions:

Preheat your air fryer to 340 degrees.

Spread your tortillas with your butter and then cook them for two to three minutes. When the tortillas are crisp take them out.

Combine your tuna, zucchini, mustard and mayonnaise in a medium bowl.

Divide your tuna, spooning I tout between their tortillas and then top it on the shredded cheese.

1. Grill them in for two to four minutes. Serve when the tuna is hot and the cheese melts and starts to brown.

Carrot Noodles

Prep Time: 5 Minutes

Cooking Time: 10 Minutes

Ingredients:

7 Large Carrots, Spiralized into Noodles

1 Tablespoon Olive Oil

¼ Teaspoon Black Pepper

½ Teaspoon Garlic Powder

2 Tablespoons Sour Cream

- 2 Tablespoons Bacon Bits

Directions:

Preheat it to 390 degrees, and put your carrot noodles into a mixing bowl.

Add in olive oil, pepper, garlic powder and sea salt. Stir it to make sure it's covered, and then place it in the air fryer.

1. Cook for ten minutes, and then top with sour cream and bacon bits before serving.

Stuffed Spinach Leaves

Prep Time: 5 Minutes

Cooking Time: 5 Minutes

Ingredients:

8 Large Spinach Leaves

1 ½ Cup Cream Cheese

1 Tablespoon Garlic Powder

¼ Teaspoon Chives

- 4 Strips Bacon, Cooked & Chopped

Directions:

Start by turning your air fryer to 390, and then mix together your bacon bits, garlic powder, chives and cream cheese.

1. Scoop it into the spinach leaves. Roll it up, and cook for four to five minutes.

Deluxe Stuffed Zucchini

Prep Time: 5-8 Minutes

Cooking Time: 8 Minutes

Ingredients:

3 Zucchinis, Large

1 Cup Pepper Jack Cheese, Shredded

1 Tablespoon Sour Cream

3 Tablespoons Breadcrumbs

1 Tablespoon Bacon Bits

¼ Teaspoon Salt

- ¼ Teaspoon Black Pepper

Directions:

Preheat to 390 degrees, and cut the ends of your zucchini off. You will then want to slice it lengthwise to form 'boats'. Scoop out the flesh from the zucchini and place the flesh in another bowl.

Put you're other ingredients in that bowl stirring to combine.

1. Spoon the mixture into your zucchini, and place in the air fryer for 8 minutes. Make sure the cheese is completely melted before serving.

Spiced Stuffed Peppers

Prep Time: 8 Minutes

Cooking Time: 12 Minutes

Ingredients:

4 Red Peppers

2 Minced Meat, Fried

3 Cups Sour Cream

1 Teaspoon Garlic Powder

¼ Teaspoon Black Pepper

- 2 Cups Cheddar Cheese, Shredded

Directions:

Slice the tops off of your red peppers and remove the inner contents.

Preheat your air fryer to 390.

Take your fried meat, sour cream, garlic, and pepper together with a large spoon.

1. Spoon the meat mixture, stuffing it into each pepper. Top it with the cheese and place it in the fryer for twelve minutes.

Spinach & Feta Pastry

Prep Time: 5 Minutes

Cooking Time: 14 Minutes

Ingredients:

4 Sheets Pastry Dough (filo is best)

2 Cups Spinach, Frozen & Thawed

2 Cloves Garlic, Chopped Fine

2 Tablespoons Olive Oil

1 Cup Feta Cheese, Crumbled

- 1 Large Egg, Beaten

Directions:

Start by preheating your fryer to 390 degrees.

Combine your garlic, cheese, spinach and olive oil in a medium bowl.

Spoon that mixture into each pastry, tucking the ends as you fold up the pastry. Brush it with egg so that the ends do mix together.

Brush the tops with olive oil, and then cut small slits into the pasties.

1. Cook for 14 minutes, and then let cool before serving.

Ham & Cheese Balls

Prep Time: 5 Minutes

Cooking Time: 15 Minutes

Ingredients:

2 Cups Buckwheat Flour

1 Cup Cooked Ham, Cubed

1 Cup Cheddar Cheese, Shredded

3 Medium Eggs, Beaten

1 Tablespoon Black Pepper

1 Teaspoon Onion Powder

¼ Teaspoon Nutmeg Powder

- 2 Tablespoons Olive Oil

Directions:

Start by heating your air fryer to 390.

Combine all ingredients together except for the olive oil.

Use the olive oil to grease and oven safe dish, and then spoon the mixture into balls before placing them in it.

1. Cook for fifteen minutes. These can be served on their own or used as a burger.

Easy Air Fryer Pizza

Prep Time: 5 Minutes

Cooking Time: 14 Minutes

Ingredients:

2 Baguettes, Sliced in Half Lengthwise

1 Cup Pizza Sauce

1 Cup Pepper Jack Cheese, shredded

1 Cup Mozzarella Cheese, Shredded

1 Green Bell Pepper, Sliced

1 Small Onion, Sliced

1. Handful Pepperoni Slices

Directions:

Start by heating your air fryer to 390.

Spread your pizza sauce on the flat side of each baguette half. Top it with cheese, green onion, bell pepper and pepperoni slices.

Place it in your air fryer basket making sure it lays flat with the topping side upward.

1. Cook for 14 minutes. The cheese should be melted, and the baguette should be crispy.

Simple Beef Burger

Prep Time: 5 Minutes

Cooking Time: 15 Minutes

Ingredients:

1 Cup Millet Flour

2 Cups Ground Beef

3 Medium Eggs

1 Teaspoon Black Pepper

1 Teaspoon Thyme

- 1 Tablespoon Garlic Powder

Directions:

Start by heating it to 390.

Combine all ingredients besides your olive oil together.

Grease an oven safe dish, and make sure that you grease it with olive oil.

Spoon the mixture into the dish, making sure to form patties.

1. Cook for fifteen minutes before taking out to cool.

Chicken a la King

Prep Time: 10 Minutes

Cooking Time: 17 Minutes

Ingredients:

2 Boneless & Skinless Chicken Breasts, Cubed

8 Button Mushrooms, Sliced

1 Red Bell Pepper, Chopped

1 Tablespoon Olive Oil

10 Ounces Refrigerated Alfredo Sauce

½ Teaspoon Thyme, Dried

6 Slices French Bread

- 2 Tablespoons Butter, Softened

Directions:

Start by heating your air fryer to 350.

Start by putting your chicken, bell pepper and mushrooms into your air fryer basket, and then drizzle with olive oil. Make sure to toss it to coat evenly.

Roast for about ten to fifteen minutes, but make sure to toss it at least once while cooking.

Remove your chicken and vegetables, placing them into a six inch metal bowl, stirring your Alfredo sauce and thyme in. return it to your air fryer and cook for another three to four minutes.

Butter your French bread slices, and when your chicken is done remove it from the basket. Add in the bread with the butter side up, and toast for two to four minutes. The bread should be lightly golden brown.

1. Place the toast on a plate and top with your chicken.

Turkey Rolls

Prep Time: 5 Minutes

Cooking Time: 10 Minutes

Ingredients:

4 Slices Turkey Breast

1 Cup Mozzarella, Fresh

1 Tomato, Sliced

½ Cup Basil, Fresh

- 4 Chive Shoots

Directions:

Preheat your air fryer to 390, and then place the slices of mozzarella, basil, and tomato on each turkey slices. Roll it up and tie it with your chive shoots.

1. Place it in your air fryer for ten minutes. It's best served with a salad.

Broccoli Bacon Burger

Prep Time: 5 Minutes

Cooking Time: 12 Minutes

Ingredients:

1 Cup Broccoli Florets, Cooked Lightly

1 Cup Potato Meal

3 Medium Eggs, Beaten

1 Cup Bacon Bits

1 Tablespoon Black Pepper

- 1 Tablespoon Olive Oil

Directions:

Start by heating your air fryer to 390 degrees, and combine all of your ingredients in a bowl. Just don't combine your olive oil.

Grease your oven safe dish using the olive oil.

Spoon your mixture into the patty form, pushing them down.

1. Cook for twelve minutes.

Turkey Stuffed Bell Pepper

Prep Time: 5 Minutes

Cooking Time: 25 Minutes

Ingredients:

1 Tablespoon Black Pepper

1 Tablespoon Olive Oil

3 Red Bell Peppers

1 Cup Cooked Turkey, Sliced

½ Cup Turkey Bacon, Chopped

1 Cup Cream Cheese

- 1 Cup Pepper Jack Cheese, Shredded

Directions:

Start by heating your air fryer to 390.

Take your red bell peppers, chopping the tops off and removing all of the seeds.

Start by taking a bowl and combining the cream cheese, turkey, bacon, and pepper. Make sure it's mixed well, and grease a pan with your olive oil.

Spoon your mixture into a bell pepper before topping it with pepper jack.

1. Cook for twenty-five minutes before serving.

Hot & Sweet Ham Sandwich

Prep Time: 15 Minutes

Cooking Time: 7 Minutes

Ingredients:

1/3 Cup Spicy Barbeque Sauce

2 Tablespoons Honey

8 Slices Bacon, Pre-cooked & Cut

1 Red Bell Pepper, Sliced Thin

1 Yellow Bell Pepper, Sliced Thin

3 Pita Pockets, Halved

1 ¼ Cups Butter Lettuce, Torn

- 2 Tomatoes, Sliced

Directions:

Start by heating it up to 350 degrees.

Next, you'll want to combine your honey and barbeque sauce. Brush your bacon slices, red and yellow bell pepper with it.

Put your peppers into your air fryer, cooking it for four minutes. Shake your basket, adding in your bacon and grilling for an additional two minutes. The bacon should be browned and the peppers should be tender.

1. Fill your pita halves with the peppers, bacon and any remaining sauce. Add in lettuce and tomato before serving.

Bean & Turkey Bacon Burger

Prep Time: 5 Minutes

Cooking Time: 20 Minutes

Ingredients:

1 Cup Black Beans, Cooked & Mashed (using a food processor is best)

4 Large Eggs, Beaten

1 Cup Turkey Bacon, Chopped

1 Cup Ground Turkey

1 Tablespoon Black Pepper

¼ Teaspoon Sea Salt

- 1 Tablespoon Olive Oil

Directions:

Start by heating your air fryer to 390.

Combine your ingredients together except for your olive oil.

Use the olive oil to grease the heat safe dish. Spoon it into a patty form.

1. Cook for twenty minutes.

Chicken Pita Sandwiches

Prep Time: 10 Minutes

Cooking Time: 10 Minutes

Ingredients:

2 Boneless, Skinless Chicken Breasts, Cubed in 1 inch Cubes

1 Small Red Onion, Sliced Thin

1 Red Bell Pepper, Sliced Thin

1/3 Cup Italian Salad Dressing

½ Teaspoon Thyme, Dried

4 Pita Pockets, Split

2 Cups Butter Lettuce, Shredded

- 1 Cup Cherry Tomatoes, Chopped

Directions:

Preheat your air fryer to 380.

Place your bell pepper, onion, and chicken into the basket of the air fryer. Drizzle Italian salad dressing on it before adding thyme and tossing it.

Bake for about nine to eleven minutes. Toss it once while it's cooking.

Transfer that chicken and vegetables to a bowl, adding in the remaining salad dressing.

1. Assemble it into your pita pockets with your tomatoes and butter lettuce.

Turkey Breast with Maple Mustard Glaze

Time: 45 minutes

Yield: 6

Ingredients:

- 5-pound of a whole turkey breast

- 1 tablespoon of olive oil

- 1 teaspoon of dried thyme

- 1 teaspoon of dried oregano

- 1 teaspoon of dried parsley

- 1 teaspoon of paprika

- 1 teaspoon of salt

- 1 teaspoon of black pepper

- ¼ cup of maple syrup

- 2 tablespoons of Dijon mustard

- **1 tablespoon of melted unsalted butter**

Instructions:

1. Preheat your air fryer to 360 degrees Fahrenheit.
2. Brush 1 tablespoon of olive oil over the turkey breast.

3. Using a small bowl, mix the dried thyme, dried oregano, dried parsley, paprika, salt, black pepper and then rub the turkey breast with the herb and spice mixture.
4. Place the seasoned turkey breast into your air fryer basket and cook it for 25 minutes.
5. After 25 minutes, flip the turkey breast and cook it for an additional 12 minutes or until the turkey is entirely done.
6. Using a saucepan, add the maple syrup, Dijon mustard and the butter, on an average temperature of heat.
7. Brush the turkey breast with the maple mustard, glaze it all over and place the back inside your air fryer.
8. Cook it for an additional 5 minutes or until the skin is crispy and brown.
9. Then remove it from your air fryer and allow it to cool off for a couple of minutes.
10. Serve and enjoy!

Nutritional Information per serving:

Calories: 180,

Fat: 1g,

Protein: 35g,

Dietary fiber: 1g,

Carbohydrates: 7g

General Wong's Beef and Broccoli

Time: 25 minutes (plus 30 minutes for marinating)

Yield: 4

Ingredients:

- 1 pound of steak, sliced into strips

- 1 pound of stemmed and chopped into florets broccoli

- 1/3 cup of oyster sauce

- 1/3 cup of sherry

- 1 tablespoon of minced ginger

- 1 tablespoon of minced garlic

- 1 tablespoon of olive oil

- 1 tablespoon of soy sauce

- 1 tablespoon of sesame oil

- **1 teaspoon of cornstarch**

Instructions:

1. Using a bowl, add the oyster sauce, sherry, minced ginger, minced garlic, olive oil, soy sauce, sesame oil, cornstarch and stir it until it is properly mixed.
2. Then, add the steak, broccoli, cover it well and allow it to marinate for 30 minutes or overnight.
3. Then preheat your air fryer to 360 degrees Fahrenheit.
4. After marinating, place the marinade steak and broccoli in your air fryer.
5. Cook it for 15 minutes at a 360 degrees Fahrenheit or until it is done.
6. Serve and enjoy along with the white rice!

Nutritional Information per serving:

Calories: 340,

Fat: 21g,

Protein: 21g,

Dietary Fiber: 2.5g,

Carbohydrates: 18g

Irresistible Meatloaf

Time: 25 minutes

Yield: 4

Ingredients:

- 1 ½ pound of lean ground beef

- 1 beaten egg

- 1 cup of panko breadcrumbs

- 1/3 cup of steak sauce

- 1 finely chopped onion

- 1 chopped green bell pepper

- ½ cup of chopped mushrooms

- 1 tablespoon of chopped thyme

- 1 teaspoon of paprika

- 1 teaspoon of garlic powder

- 1 teaspoon of salt

- **1 teaspoon of black pepper**

Instructions:

1. Preheat your air fryer to 390 degrees Fahrenheit.
2. Using a large bowl, add all the ingredients and stir until it mixes properly.
3. Thereafter, grease a heat-safe pan or the air fryer baking accessory with a nonstick cooking spray.
4. Add the mixed ground beef into the pan or baking accessory and flatten the top.
5. After that, place the pan or accessory inside your air fryer and cook it for 25 minutes at a 390 degrees Fahrenheit or until it gets brown and done.
6. Thereafter, carefully remove it from your air fryer and allow it to cool off before serving.
7. Serve and enjoy!

Nutritional Information per serving:

Calories: 300,

Fat: 18g,

Protein: 23g,

Dietary fiber: 0.7g,

Carbohydrates: 9g

Rockstar Rib Eye-Steak

Time: 20 minutes

Yield: 1 or 2

Ingredients:

- 2 pounds of rib-eye steak

- 1 tablespoon of olive oil

- 1 teaspoon of salt

- 1 teaspoon of black pepper

- 1 teaspoon of ground coriander

- 1 teaspoon of brown sugar

- 1 teaspoon of sweet paprika

- 1 teaspoon of mustard powder

- 1 teaspoon of onion powder

- 1 teaspoon of chili powder

- **1 teaspoon of garlic powder**

Instructions:

1. Preheat your air fryer to 390 degrees Fahrenheit.
2. Sprinkle the olive oil over the rib-eye steak.
3. Season the steak on all sides with all the listed seasonings until it is well covered.
4. Place the steak into your air fryer basket.
5. Cook it for 8 minutes at a 390 degrees Fahrenheit.
6. After 8 minutes, flip the steak over and cook for an additional 7 minutes.
7. When done, carefully remove the steak from your air fryer and allow it to cool off before serving.
8. Serve and enjoy!

Nutritional Information per serving:

Calories: 520,

Fat: 35g,

Dietary Fiber: 0g,

Carbohydrates: 2g,

Protein: 56g

25. Unimaginable Zucchini Bacon Lasagna

Time: 30 minutes

Yield: 4

Ingredients:

- 2 thinly sliced zucchinis

- 6 strips of bacon

- 2 cups of grated ricotta cheese

- 2 cups of grated mozzarella cheese

- 2 teaspoons of onion powder

- 1 teaspoon of garlic powder

- 1 teaspoon of salt

- **1 teaspoon of black pepper**

Instructions:

1. Preheat your air fryer to 390 degrees Fahrenheit.
2. Grease a lasagna pan with a nonstick cooking spray.
3. Using a bowl, add and mix the ricotta cheese, mozzarella cheese, onion powder, garlic powder, salt, and the black pepper properly.
4. Cut the zucchini into layers and place it in the lasagna pan.
5. Add the seasoned cheese mixture.
6. Then, add the bacon and sprinkle it with the seasoned cheese.
7. Repeat this again by layering the zucchini, cheese, bacon, until all the ingredients has been used.
8. Place the lasagna pan in your oven and cook it for 15 minutes or until the cheese gets melted.

9. Serve and enjoy!

Nutritional Information per serving:

Calories: 335,

Fat: 12g,

Protein: 16g,

Dietary Fiber: 5g,

Carbohydrates: 40g

Fantastic Garlic Butter Pork Chops

Time: 20 minutes

Yield: 4

Ingredients:

- 4 pork chops

- ¼ cup of melted butter

- 1 tablespoon of olive oil

- 4 minced garlic cloves

- 2 tablespoons of thinly sliced parsley

- 1 teaspoon of salt

- **1 teaspoon of black pepper**

Instructions:

1. Preheat your air fryer to 360 degrees Fahrenheit.
2. Using a bowl, add and mix all the ingredients except for the pork chops properly.

3. Brush the mixture on all the dimensions of the pork sides.
4. Grease your air fryer and place it on the pork chops inside.
5. Cook it for 7 minutes at a 360 degrees Fahrenheit.
6. After 7 minutes, flip the pork chops and cook it for an additional 7 minutes.
7. Serve and enjoy!

Nutritional Information per serving:

Calories: 200,

Fat: 6g,

Protein: 20g,

Dietary Fiber: 0.2g,

Carbohydrates: 18g

Super-Yummy Roast Pork Belly

Time:

Yield: 2

Ingredients:

- 2 pounds of pork belly

- 2 teaspoons of garlic powder

- 2 teaspoons of onion powder

- 1 teaspoon of smoked paprika

- 1 teaspoon of salt

- 2 teaspoons of five-spice powder

- 2 teaspoons of rosemary

- **1 teaspoon of black pepper**

Instructions:

1. Fill a large pot with enough water, boil it and then add the pork belly into the hot water for 10 minutes.
2. Then remove it from the boiling water and allow it to dry for 3 hours or until it dries completely.
3. Use a fork to poke some holes all around the pork belly.
4. While still doing that, using a small mixing bowl, add and mix all the seasonings together, then rub the pork belly with the seasonings.
5. Preheat your air fryer to 320 degrees Fahrenheit.
6. Place the pork belly inside your air fryer and cook it for 30 minutes.
7. Increase the temperature to 360 degrees Fahrenheit and cook it for an additional 20 minutes.
8. Serve and enjoy!

Nutritional Information per serving:

Calories: 240,

Fat: 20g,

Protein: 13g,

Dietary Fiber: 0g,

Carbohydrates: 1g

Outstanding Rack of Lamb

Time: 25 minutes

Yield: 4

Ingredients:

- 2 racks of lamb

- ¼ cup of freshly chopped parsley

- 4 cloves of minced garlic

- 2 tablespoons of olive oil

- 2 tablespoons of honey

- 1 teaspoon of salt

- **1 teaspoon of black pepper**

Instructions:

1. Preheat your air fryer to 390 degrees Fahrenheit.
2. Using a blender or food processor, add the parsley, garlic cloves, olive oil, honey, salt, and black pepper and blend it until it gets totally grounded.
3. Rub the grounded parsley-garlic on the lamb racks, without using them all as you will need them later.
4. Put the grill pan accessory into your air fryer, and place the lamb racks on top.
5. Cook it for 15 minutes at a 390 degrees Fahrenheit or until it gets brown in color.
6. Spread another layer of the puree on the lamb racks.
7. Serve and enjoy!

Nutritional Information per serving:

Calories: 335,

Fat: 26g,

Protein: 21g,

Dietary Fiber: 0g,

Carbohydrates: 2.5g

Phenomenal Herbed Roast Beef

Time: 1 hour

Yield: 4

Ingredients:

- 4-pound roasted beef

- 1 tablespoon of olive oil

- 1 teaspoon of salt

- 1 teaspoon of black pepper

- 1 teaspoon of dried thyme

- 1 tablespoon of freshly chopped rosemary

- **1 tablespoon of freshly chopped parsley**

Instructions:

1. Preheat your air fryer to 360 degrees Fahrenheit.
2. Using a bowl, add and mix the olive oil, salt, black pepper, thyme, rosemary, parsley properly.
3. Rub the mixture all over the roasted beef.
4. Place the beef inside your air fryer basket and cook it for 20 minutes.
5. After 20 minutes, flip the beef over and cook for an additional 30 minutes or until it reaches your desired preference.
6. Remove the roasted beef and allow it to cool of before serving.
7. Serve and enjoy!

Nutritional Information per serving:

Calories: 210,

Fat: 10g,

Protein: 27g,

Dietary Fiber: 0.2g,

Carbohydrates: 0.6g

Remarkable Air-Fried Ham with Honey and Brown Sugar Glaze

Time: 1 hour

Yield: 6

Ingredients:

- 4-pound of fully cooked slice ham

- 1 cup of pineapple juice

- 1 cup of brown sugar

- ½ cup of honey

- 2 orange juice

- **1 teaspoon of salt**

Instructions:

1. Preheat your air fryer to 350 degrees Fahrenheit.
2. Grease your air fryer basket with a nonstick cooking spray and add the 4-pound ham or a big sized ham that can fit properly into your air fryer.
3. Cook the ham for 15 minutes at a 350 degrees Fahrenheit.
4. While still doing that, using a saucepan, add and mix 1 cup of pineapple juice, 1 cup of brown sugar, ½ cup of honey, the 2 orange juices, and 1 teaspoon of salt properly.

5. Simmer the pineapple-glaze mixture using an average temperature of heat until the glaze has thickened.
6. After the 15 minutes has elapsed, open your air fryer and pour half of the glaze on top of the ham. Cook the ham for an additional 25 minutes inside your air fryer at a 350 degrees or until it is done.
7. Once its done, carefully remove the ham from your air fryer and pour the remaining half of the sauce over.
8. Serve and enjoy!

Nutritional Information per serving:

Calories: 180,

Fat: 0.7g,

Dietary Fiber: 0.5g,

Carbohydrates: 38g,

Protein: 4g

Amazing Lamb Chops with Herbed Garlic Sauce

Time: 25 minutes

Yield: 4

Ingredients:

- 4 lamb chops

- 1 garlic bulb

- 1 tablespoon of freshly chopped parsley

- 1 tablespoon of freshly chopped oregano

- 2 tablespoons of olive oil

- 1 teaspoon of onion powder

- 1 teaspoon of salt

- **1 teaspoon of black pepper**

Instructions:

1. Preheat your air fryer to 390 degrees Fahrenheit.
2. Brush the garlic bulb with an olive oil and place it inside your air fryer,cook it for 12 minutes or until it is properly roasted, then remove it from your air fryer and set it aside.
3. Using a small bowl, mix the parsley, oregano, olive oil, onion powder, salt, and the black pepper properly.
4. Thereafter spread each lamb chop with about one teaspoon of the herbed olive oil mixture.
5. Place the lamb chops into your air fryer and cook it for 6 minutes at a 390 degrees Fahrenheit or until it turns brown.
6. Press the garlic cloves with a garlic press and mix it properly with the herbed olive oil.
7. Spread the garlic sauce over the lamb chops.
8. Serve and enjoy!

Nutritional Information per serving:

Calories: 180,

Fat: 8g,

Protein: 23g,

Carbohydrates: 1.7g,

Dietary Fiber: 0.5g

Roasted Lamb Rack with a Macadamia Crust

Total Time: 60 minutes

Ingredients

- 1 3/4 pound (28oz) rack of lamb
- 1 tablespoon olive oil
- 1 garlic clove, finely chopped
- Salt and pepper

Macadamia Crust

- 1 tablespoon breadcrumbs
- 3oz unsalted macadamia nuts
- 1 tablespoon chopped fresh rosemary
- 1 egg

Directions

1. Combine the olive oil and chopped garlic to create the garlic oil. Brush the lamb rack with the oil and season with salt and pepper.

2. Preheat the air fryer to 220°F/104ºC. Finely chop the nuts and place in a bowl. Blend in the breadcrumbs and rosemary. Whip the egg in another bowl.

3. Coat the lamb by dipping the meat into the whipped egg, draining off any excess, then coat the lamb with the macadamia crust.

4. Place the coated lamb rack in the cooking basket, slide in and set the timer for 30 minutes.

5. After 30 minutes has elapsed, increase the temperature to 390°F/198ºC and set the timer for a few minutes.

6. Remove the meat and allow to rest, covered with aluminum foil, for 10 minutes before serving.

Air Fryer Meatballs

Preparation time: 10 minutes

Ingredients

- 2 cups ground beef

- 1 bunch coriander leaves, chopped
- 2 bread slices
- 1 onion, chopped
- ¼ teaspoon black pepper
- ½ teaspoon salt
- 1 teaspoon garlic pate
- 1 teaspoon ginger powder
- 1 teaspoon cumin powder
- ¼ teaspoon cinnamon powder

Directions

1. In a food processor add beef, bread slices, coriander, salt, pepper, cumin powder, cinnamon powder, and ginger garlic paste. Blend well.
2. Grease your hands with some oil and make small round balls with mixture.
3. Preheat fryer at 360 F.
4. Transfer meatballs into fryer basket and let to cook for 8 minutes on 360 F.
5. After that cook for 5 minutes on 330 F.

Marinated Rosemary Zest Turkey Breast

Preparation time: 45 minutes

Ingredients

- 1 turkey breast
- 3 tablespoons honey
- 1 teaspoon garlic powder
- ¼ teaspoon black pepper
- ½ teaspoon salt
- 2 tablespoons rosemary, chopped
- 2 tablespoons lemon juice
- 1 teaspoon cinnamon powder

Directions

1. In a medium bowl add, garlic powder, honey, lemon juice, black pepper, cinnamon powder, rosemary, and salt. Mix to combine.
2. Drizzle over turkey breast and toss rub all over gently. Let to marinade for 30 minutes.
3. Preheat air fryer at 360 F.

4. Now place turkey breast into fryer basket as much can fit and let to cook for 22 minutes at 360 F.

5. Transfer to serving platter.

Honey Glazed Pork Ribs

Preparation time: 7 minutes

Ingredients

- 4 oz. pork ribs
- ½ cup honey
- 2 tablespoons soya sauce
- 1 teaspoon black pepper
- ½ teaspoon salt
- 1 teaspoon garlic paste

Directions

1. In a piping bag add honey, soya sauce, black pepper, salt, garlic and pork ribs, and shake bag to coat well.

2. Preheat air fryer at 360 F.

3. Transfer pork ribs and leave to cook for 7 minutes.

Air Fryer Baked Beef and Potatoes

Preparation time: 15 minutes

Ingredients

- 4 oz. beef cut into bite pieces
- 3 potatoes, peeled, diced
- 1 onion, sliced
- ¼ teaspoon chili powder
- ½ teaspoon salt
- 2 tablespoons soya sauce
- 2 garlic cloves, minced
- 1 tablespoon olive oil
- 1 tablespoon coriander leaves, chopped

Directions

1. In air fryer add beef, potatoes, garlic, soya sauce, oil, salt and chili powder. Mix to combine.
2. Let to cook for 8 minutes on 360 F.

3. Now add onion and cook again for 8 minutes on 330 F.

4. Transfer to serving dish and sprinkle coriander on top.

Spicy Masala Boti

Preparation time: 35 minutes

Ingredients

- 4 oz. beef, boneless, cut into small pieces
- 1 teaspoon dry coriander powder
- 1 teaspoon cinnamon powder
- 1 teaspoon cumin powder
- 1 teaspoon cayenne pepper
- 2 tablespoons vinegar
- ½ teaspoon salt
- 1 teaspoon garlic powder
- 1 teaspoon ginger powder
- 1 teaspoon olive oil

Directions

1. In a bowl add all spices and mix to combine.

2. Transfer beef into fryer and sprinkle all spices, mix well to combine.

3. Now add vinegar and olive oil and toss well.

4. Leave to cook for 15 minutes on 390 F.

5. After that cook for 5 minutes on 360 F.

Crispy Pork Roast

Preparation time: 10 minutes

Ingredients

- 2-3 pork chops
- 1 tablespoon garlic powder
- 1 tablespoon ginger powder
- 1 egg, whisked
- 1 cup bread crumbs
- ¼ cup flour
- 1 teaspoon onion powder
- 1 teaspoon black pepper
- ½ teaspoon salt

Directions

1. In a bowl combine flour, breadcrumbs, salt, pepper, ginger powder, garlic powder and onion powder. Mix well.

2. Dip each pork chop into egg then roll out into bread crumbs mixture.

3. Transfer pork into air fryer basket and let to cook for 6 minutes.

4. Flip the sides and now leave to cook for 4 minutes on 150 F.

Hot Shot Factions

Preparation time: 22 minutes

Ingredients

- 4 oz. beef steaks, cut into 2 inch pieces
- ½ cup tomato ketchup
- 2 tablespoons vinegar
- 2 tablespoons honey
- ½ teaspoon salt

- ¼ teaspoon garlic paste
- 2 tablespoons lime juice

Directions

2. Take a bowl and add, tomato ketchup, honey, garlic paste, salt, and lime juice.

3. Mix to combine.

5. Transfer into air fryer at 360 F for 22 minutes.

Conclusion

The air fryer is an innovative kitchen appliance that you need if you want to cook your food using less oil. If you want to eat healthy meals that are big on flavor and nutrients but are low in fat, then the air fryer is for you.

Reasons You Need an Air Fryer

1. It uses less oil.

An air fryer utilizes rapidly circulating air that is heated up to 390 degrees Fahrenheit to cook all kinds of food instead of dunking them deep in fat. This technology "fries" chicken, fish, chips, pastries, and your other favorite food by heating up the ingredients you use from all sides at the same time. Food prepared with the air fryer turn out perfectly crisp and browned on the outside yet tender and moist inside, even without using lots of fat.

2. It cooks food evenly.

The cooking chamber of the air fryer emits heat close to the food you place in the air fryer basket, which helps you cook more efficiently. Meanwhile, its exhaust fan (on top of the cooking chamber) provides the airflow needed to pass through the ingredients from the underside. The air fryer also supplies constant heating temperature on all sides of the food, helping further ensure that your food cooks evenly.

3. It provides convenience without sacrificing flavor.

A wide tray that you can easily remove is installed in the air fryer, which can serve up hot and crispy food within just twelve minutes. Your food ends up having fewer calories and healthier at that because you only need small amounts of fat to cook it, but still has that "fried" taste and texture.

4. It gives you peace of mind.

Even though the air fryer uses superheated air to cook your food, it does come with a cooling system together with a motor axis mounted fan that controls the temperature inside the appliance. This helps keep the cooking chamber sanitary and healthy, especially since the cooling system also lets fresh air move through the air fryer's filters and bottom side. The same fresh air also helps prevent all internal parts of the air fryer from heating up too much.

Air Fryer Cooking Tips

1. Use oil sprays.

Oil sprays make it easy for you to use less oil when cooking your favorite food. Compared to brushing or drizzling, spraying is a better way to apply oil evenly on food. You can also use oil sprays to coat the air fryer basket's bottom side to prevent any ingredients from sticking to it.

2. Preheat the air fryer.

This is an important step you have to make prior to putting your food in the air fryer. You simply set the appliance to the temperature called for in a particular recipe, then set the timer to go off after 2 to 3 minutes. You will know that your food is ready to be loaded into the air fryer basket once the timer is set off.

3. Discard the fat.

You may need to take out the air fryer basket at times to empty any fat that accumulates, especially after cooking chicken wings and other food that naturally contain high amounts of fat.

4. Add water.

It helps to moisten the drawer below the air fryer basket when air-frying fatty food as this helps in keeping the grease from becoming too hot to the point of smoking. Simply fill the drawer with water when air-frying burgers, sausages, or bacon.

5. Apply breading properly.

When cooking food that needs breading, it would be wise to coat them in small batches and press the breading properly. This ensures that the breading is evenly applied and more likely to adhere to the food. Your air fryer has a powerful fan attached to its mechanism. At times, the fan can blow the breading off the food, and this can prevent excess smoke from passing through the exhaust filter.

6. Avoid overcrowding the basket.

Doing so will help ensure that the air inside your air fryer circulates well. Otherwise, your food does not get cooked properly and your cooking time is prolonged.

7. Shake it.

This will help re-distribute the food as well as cook, brown, and make them evenly crispy.

8. Make use of toothpicks.

Toothpicks are great for holding food down. The air fryer fan can pick up light food such as bread slices on sandwiches.

9. Flip your food.

Doing this halfway through your cooking time will help a lot in having your food browned evenly on all sides.

10. Use foil correctly.

There are air fryer recipes that call for being covered with aluminum foil or parchment paper. The problem with this is that the steam cannot pass easily, which is why you need to trim the foil or paper so that there is a half-inch space around the air fryer basket's bottom edge.

11. Pat dry before cooking.

To keep food from splattering and creating excessive smoke (this is especially true for marinated food and other ingredients pre-soaked in liquid), it is best to pat them dry with paper towels first.

12. Make use of any juices left.

Juices, drippings, and excess marinades can be left behind by certain food, and they are collected by the drawer beneath the air fryer basket. Don't throw them away; you can use them as a sauce to add more flavor to your cooked food.

13. Soak before cleaning.

It helps soak the air fryer basket in soapy water after each use. This ensures that any remaining food particles are loosened and removed completely.

14. Use the proper aids.

It helps to invest on a number of kitchen accessories to help you air-fry your food more efficiently. Oven-safe cake pans and baking dishes will come in handy when cooking in the air fryer. Just keep them from being in direct contact with the appliance's heating element and make sure to buy only those accessories that you can easily load inside the basket in the air fryer.

15. Know the right location.

It is important that you have the proper location for your air fryer. Keep it on a heat-resistant, level countertop at all times. You also need to see to it that the back of the air fryer is located at least 5 inches away from the exhaust vent.

Printed in Great Britain
by Amazon